WHAT WOULD KINKY DO?

St. Martin's Press
New York

WHAT WOULD KINKY DO?

HOW TO UNSCREW A SCREWED-UP WORLD

KINKY FRIEDMAN

Cartoons by John Callahan

Drawings copyright by John Callahan.

Some of the pieces in this book have appeared in various forms in *Texas
Monthly, Rolling Stone, American Airlines* magazine, *New York Post, The
Scottish Times, The L.A. Times,* and *The New York Times.*

"Willy the Wandering Gypsy and Me" and "Jesus Was Our Savior," by Billy
Joe Shaver, copyright© 1972 Sony/ATV Songs LLC (renewed). All rights ad-
ministered by Sony/ATV Music Publishing, 8 Music Square West, Nashville,
TN, 37203. All rights reserved. Used by permission.

Library of Congress Cataloging-in-Publication Data

Friedman, Kinky.
    What would Kinky do? : how to unscrew a screwed-up world / Kinky
Friedman.—1st ed.
        p. cm.
    ISBN-13: 978-0-312-33159-7
    ISBN-10: 0-312-33159-2
    I. Title.
    PS3556.R527W46 2008
    814'.54—dc22

                                                        2008012736

First Edition: July 2008

10 9 8 7 6 5 4 3 2 1

Dedicated to LePetomane,

Who brought a breath of fresh air

To Europe

And never touched cloth

CONTENTS

PART IV ⁎ Advice on Going on a Journey

163

PART V ⁎ Advice on Coming Home   **215**

ACKNOWLEDGMENTS

Thanks to George Witte and Terra Gerstner at St. Martin's Press, and David Vigliano, agent. Thanks, also, to Sage Ferrero and Max Swafford.

As for the rest of the world, I simply offer the Reverend Goat Carson's Native American Thanksgiving prayer: Thanks for nothing.

A MESSAGE FROM THE AUTHOR

Regarding the Artist

The art and illustrations for this book were created by the world-famous, widely syndicated, often praised, often vilified, paralyzed genius, John Callahan. How does he come up with the ideas? I told you. He's a fucking genius. But how, might you ask, does he actually draw the illustrations? I'll let Callahan tell you in his own words: "I clutch the pen between both hands in a pathetic, childlike manner that endears me to millions of conflicted fans around the world."

The author is highly gratified that the illustrations for this book are the creations of the brilliantly sick John Callahan, one of the few modern American artists worthy of the name. Callahan's work is imbued with a rare, primitive, visceral integrity that often creates in me a mild state of sexual arousal.

There are a number of instances, indeed, when Callahan's art so perfectly mates with my prose that it is cause for celebration, and, perhaps quite understandably, causes many to masturbate like a monkey at the zoo.

John Callahan also writes songs. Many people like to sing and record John's songs. He has recently released a new CD that contains one of my favorite Callahan tunes, "Purple Winos in the Rain." As Waylon Jennings once told me, if I had a session tonight I'd cut it. Unfortunately, I haven't had a session in almost twenty-five years, unless you want to count a recent session with a large Bulgarian masseuse.

What Would Kinky Do?, liberally decorated with Callahan droppings, should provide an entertaining diversion for the many among us who suffer from suicidal depression and whose lives are spiraling downward into tailspins of despair. Others, suffering from Attention Deficit Disorder, may find John Callahan's offerings enjoyable as well. And as for the rest of us? What the hell. Somewhere in all this horseshit there's got to be a pony.

WHAT WOULD KINKY DO?

INTRODUCTION

L et us begin this ordeal with a fairly safe assumption: No human being who has ever lived in this world has ever taken good advice. Millions upon millions of people, however, have gladly and gratefully taken bad advice, foolish advice, pop advice, and glib advice. Why is this? No doubt it's partly because of the perversity of human nature. This notwithstanding, the other part, I believe, is because of the sanctimonious, constipated, pompous, smug, and self-righteous way that good advice is usually given.

This is the main reason most people reject good advice and instead ask themselves, What would Jesus do? Or, What would Ernest Tubb do? Or, What would Will Rogers do? In their time, these folks probably asked their own version of the same question. Jesus indubitably asked, What would My Father do? Ernest Tubb might have wondered, What would Jimmie Rodgers do? And Will Rogers no doubt asked, What would Mark Twain do? This way you avoid dealing with the sermonizing, patronizing, advice-giver altogether; you merely find someone you would like to be like when you grow up and cut right to the chase.

This is why I have assiduously avoided giving any direct good advice in this book. Had I attempted to do so, sure as hell, it would've been summarily rejected by you, gentile reader. Instead, I have tried to cleverly couch anything I deem to be good advice within a deceptive, deviously designed delivery system, i.e., humor, misdirection, and, of course, lots and lots of common Zen bullshit.

I have come to believe that good advice, like ragtag, weatherbeaten human wisdom of any kind, can only be delivered or received obliquely, accidentally, intuitively. Few of us want the hard truth these days anyway. Mankind never has wanted to deal with that. So if you want a religion that still makes you think you're a good Christian even though you own ten homes and fifty cars, you've come to the wrong book.

What would Donald Trump do? What would Bill Gates do? For answers, look at Columbus reaching the Bank of America. Look at the sad, narrow-casted, Starbucked world all around you. There are many people in the world today whom we would call important; there are precious few, indeed, whom we might consider truly significant. If your goal is to make a lot of money and have a lot of power and that's all you really care about,

"Well, it looks like the guests are beginning to trickle in."

you're a shallow, mean-minded, vacuous excuse for a human being and I don't want you reading this book anyway. Stop, before it's too late. You're wasting your time and my time and time is the money of love.

If, on the other hand, you're the kind of person who feels it might be nice to marry a prostitute, contract syphilis, kill yourself between two rows of corn, and leave a lasting legacy of love and truth and beauty, then you might ask yourself, What would Vincent van Gogh do? You might also ask yourself, Where did Vincent van Go? That one, I can answer for you. He went into the creation of what Emily Dickinson called "the thing with feathers that perches in the soul." That would be a little thing called hope. He also went into the unconscious construction of what we call "the still, small voice within." That would be our conscience, which may not be the voice of God but it's close enough for country dancin'. Finally, he went to the heart of all mankind's dearest, desperate, diaper-driving dreams.

By this time, it should be clear to most readers that this introduction, as well as the book itself, was largely ghostwritten by Mary Higgins Clark. I've got a lot on my plate right now and I can't be concerned with casting my soul into purgatory and hoping some three-headed dog will catch the frisbee. I want to live! I want to paint! I want to finish this fucking introduction!

So please, do not ask, What would Kinky do? Because that, my friends, depends on you.

PART I

Advice on Life, Death, and Everything in Between

UNFAIR GAME

Since I've forgotten the first half of my life, it's rather difficult for me to remember my childhood, but I do recall going hunting at the wise old age of seven for the first and last time. One night my four-year-old brother, Roger, and I went coon hunting near Medina with our neighbor Cabbie. Cabbie had an old coon dog named Rip, and Roger suggested that I kiss the dog on the nose. It was the last time in my life I ever took advice from anyone who is younger than I am. Rip bit me ferociously on *my* nose, causing excessive bleeding and even more excessive tears.

Eventually, the hunt proceeded with Cabbie navigating his Jeep down by a stream under a canopy of beautiful cypress trees. It was a dark, moonless night, and Cabbie told us to look up at the tops of the trees and squeeze the trigger when we saw a pair of eyes. This seemingly simple suggestion was complicated somewhat by the fact that God had chosen that night to envelop the Hill Country in a majestic cathedral sky from which stars peripatetically peeped out through the branches at little children, making it impossible to determine whether you were shooting a raccoon or a star. In the end my brother and I each killed a young ringtail, an animal officially recognized as a varmint by the county. We collected a bounty of $1.50 apiece. We did not inquire back then, nor did the county ever tell us, what bounty they might have offered for killing a star.

Now, you might be asking yourself, "Why is this man sifting through the ashes of his childhood for a poignant hunting story now that hunting season is over?" The answer is that hunting season is never really over. Deer season may have ended, but that does not mean any of us are safe from an errant bullet fired by an errant bullethead. It only means that hunters have turned their cold sights from harmless Bambies and creatures that fly higher than their dreams to other prey. There is never a moment when a Texan cannot legally curl his finger 'round a happy trigger. Seasons have been decreed for white-tailed deer, mule deer, pronghorn antelope, alligator, dove, turkey, rabbit, javelina, quail, pheasant, squirrel, and yes, Virginia, that most fearsome of all predators in the wild, the lesser prairie chicken.

Today, however, I do not suffer hunters gladly. I realize, of course, that in a deeper sense all of us are hunting for something, and few of us ever find it. If we do, we often find ourselves killing the thing we love. As Oscar Wilde once so aptly described fox hunting: "The unspeakable in pursuit of the inedible." And yet it goes on and on. Dressed in camouflage, the great white hunters sit in family restaurants, shiver in deer blinds, and swap stories sometimes proud, sometimes wistful, for the one that got away. As blameless as bullfighters and butterfly collectors, these men for all seasons continue to wage a one-sided war against creation. They hunt only, they say, to cull the vast deer population. They hunt only to teach kids how to hunt. These are the good reasons they give, but they are not necessarily the real reasons. The truth is a much more difficult animal to track. As an honest old redneck once told me about deer: "I just like to put the brakes on 'em."

Yet ours is not the only culture lacking enough culture not to practice such practices. In my own Peace Corps experience in Borneo, I lived for a time among a nomadic tribe of pygmies known as the Punan. One of the delicacies of the Punan is monkey brains, which I ate on a number of occasions. Monkey brains, perhaps not surprisingly, taste quite similar to lesser prairie chicken. The Punan use blowpipes to kill their game, but these seemingly primitive little people are not without their own values of sportsmanship. They do not shoot an animal until it has seen them coming, which gives their prey a fighting chance to flee. This is a foreign concept to those more civilized Texans who hunt elk from a helicopter.

Fortunately, only about 4 percent of all Texans are licensed hunters. This means that 96 percent of us are relegated to the unhappy status of moving targets. Once the hunters shoot the donkey in the farmer's field, they'll shoot our asses next. A great writer named Anonymous once wrote: "The larger the prey, the more corrupt is the soul of the hunter." This may help explain why so many big-game hunters suffer from erectile dysfunction and run the risk of ending up like Ernest Hemingway, who eventually bagged the biggest game of all, himself. If you live in the Hill Country, however, you're probably just proud to have survived another hunting season without getting your head blown off. This does not necessarily guarantee, of course, that you won't be shot in the buttocks by some bow-hunting nerd.

ARRIVEDERCI
MELANOMÁ

I was just a small boy when our family dentist in Houston told my father it was imperative that he have his wisdom teeth taken out immediately. Fifty years later, my dad had them removed. My old-timer friend Earl Buckelew once told me he never paid any mind to cholesterol. "Hell," he said, "when we were growin' up, we didn't even know we had blood." My own attitude toward health matters has been pretty similar. In Hawaii and Australia, I've rarely bothered to apply suntan lotion unless it was to a shapely pair of legs obviously not belonging to me. In other words, I never gave much thought to saving my own skin. Then, things suddenly got serious as cancer.

Before my typewriter and I drown ourselves in intimations of morality, let me say for the record that I'm not a hypochondriac,

"My technique for rectal examination is somewhat different in that I'm gay and have no arms."

nor do I believe every word a doctor tells me. I've always possessed the two qualities that Ingrid Bergman claimed were essential to happiness: good health and bad memory. (At least I *think* it was Ingrid Bergman.) The fact is, sometimes if you ignore what a doctor tells you, everything will be fine. Other times you can answer that knock on the door and it's an old man with a scythe selling Girl Scout cookies.

At any rate, when I was in Austin a few months back, I noticed that parts of my anatomy were beginning to resemble those of an ancient sea tortoise. My Kerrville dermatologist, Fred Speck (I always thought Dr. Speck was a good name for a dermatologist), has a rather long waiting list, so I went to a new guy, Tom Yturri, a physician's assistant recommended to me by a doctor friend of my fairy godmother's. When I showed Yturri what was troubling me, he waved his hand and said it was nothing, but he did find two or three other little spots that piqued his curiosity. He brought in another guy, Dr. Kevin Flynn, who was wearing a rather elaborate pair of scuba goggles, and they studied the spots together.

"We'll do biopsies on these three," Yturri said at last.

"Let me guess," I said. "Whether you do two or three depends on how far behind you are on your boat payments?"

Yturri chuckled dryly. He did the biopsies fairly painlessly, putting each specimen into a separate little bottle like Dr. Quincy used to do on TV. Quincy was a coroner, of course, so his patients rarely made wisecracks.

"We'll call you in a few weeks," Yturri said. "Don't worry. It's probably nothing."

That was when I started to worry—and for good reason. Four days later, Yturri called to say that the spot on my shoulder was a melanoma. Very bad. The spot under my right eye was something that sounded like a "Sasquatch," which I'd always thought was an abominable snowman. Also very bad. Both of them, along with my wallet, had to be surgically removed right away. The spot on my right arm, apparently, was benign.

Why me? I'd never been perfect, but at least I'd been God-fearing enough to avoid going to temple. And what the hell was a melanoma, anyway? Like most Americans, I had no idea, although I knew I didn't want one. Fortunately, Roscoe West, formerly of the Texas Jewboys, was my housepest at the ranch that weekend. His brother, he said, had once had a melanoma. "Is he still with us?" I asked.

"No," Roscoe said.

"I see," I said, as I swallowed my cigar.

I also talked with people who knew someone with a melanoma who'd survived and had never been visited with skin cancer again. All this put me through some rather wild mood swings, at times causing me to feel almost at death's door. I'd tell friends about my situation, and they'd say, "Oh, I'm so sorry." This response did little to lift my spirits. At other times, however, I found myself in a surprisingly good mood. Fighting cancer, I thought, might help lend focus to my otherwise unstructured life. It might give me something I'd never really had before: a hobby.

On the day of my surgery, I met with two doctors: Aravind Sankar, from India by way of Los Angeles, and Patti Huang, from Taiwan by way of North Carolina. I came from Northwest Austin by way of pickup truck. "This ain't what's going to get you, Kinky," Dr. Sankar assured me. "The melanoma is very superficial."

"So am I," I told him. "But I don't want to die before the next Yanni concert."

In a small bed in a small room, wearing a hospital smock, I watched a young nurse try to put a needle in my arm for the IV. A fifteen-year-old from a local high school was standing by taking copious notes.

"Damn!" I said, after being jabbed repeatedly to no avail.

"Please don't curse," the nurse said officiously.

"What the hell?" I said, paraphrasing my father. "I can't say 'damn' in front of a c–h–i–l–d?"

I was angry. The one thing I didn't need was a young person

who couldn't put in an IV giving me a morality lecture just moments before I was to be wheeled into surgery. Luckily, a major tension convention was avoided. Another person came in, put in the IV, and before I knew it, I was in the operating room.

Dr. Huang would be cutting on my face, apparently, at the same time that Dr. Sankar would be carving up my shoulder. Dr. Sankar introduced me to the anesthesiologist, whom he referred to as "the bartender." After that, it all seemed like a normal evening at the Continental Club. Later, Dr. Sankar told me that I'd really cracked up the operating room as I was coming to. Evidently, someone had asked me a question about my having been in the Peace Corps. My response, according to the good doctor, was that my penis had been cut off in Borneo.

At this writing, I'm happy to say that I'm alive and well and freely dispensing advice to wear sunscreen, a big hat, and a long-sleeved shirt, and to see your dermatologist regularly. In the case of old farts like myself, however, the damage was done long ago, and young people probably won't listen anyway. Health, after all, is merely the slowest possible rate at which we die.

The good news is that skin cancer is rarely fatal if caught early. I do have two little tips to share with you, both of which have worked for me. The first is to do what Michael Jackson does: Hire a guy to follow you around with an umbrella. If that doesn't work, try singing that cheerful old John Denver song, "Melanoma on my shoulder makes me happy."

A POCKET GUIDE TO MULLETS

The humble mullet has been around since the dawn of man. Modern-day scientists speculate that Homo erectus were the first humanoids to actively cultivate mullets; in fact, the oldest known mullet was rumored to have been discovered in a tar pit next to bag of pork rinds and a fossilized Iron Maiden album. It is argued that the mullet has endured where other creatures have fallen extinct because it is able to adapt to its environment, fluidly shifting and shaping itself like a Kentucky waterfall.

After deciding to acquire a mullet, the first question the new mullet owner must ask is, "What kind of mullet do I want?" Even though, like a snowflake, mullets are all different and beautiful, there are many distinct subspecies to choose from. In this pocket guide to mullets, I will describe mullets you may encounter during your hunt.

MULLET SUBSPECIES

The 10–90: The truest form of the mullet, it contains 10 percent of hair on top and 90 percent in the back. The majority of famous mullets fall into this category: Jesus, Buffalo Bill, MacGyver, Patrick Swayze, Paul McCartney, Luke Skywalker, Billy Ray Cyrus, Captain Planet. This is the father of all mullets and from its loins sprang all the following subspecies.

The Crimullet: Favored by prison inmates, this is very similar in appearance to a classic mullet; the only difference is that this mullet will seldom, if ever, experience the sweet taste of freedom. Thumb through any prison's mugshot album and you'll find a whole herd of them.

The Drullet: The dreadlock mullet is an exotic blend of mullet and dreadlock. The Drullet is not often seen in America; the most famous one is sported by English footballer Rio Ferdinand. Acquiring one of these may prove expensive due to its rarity.

The Dykemullet: Dykemullets are intimidating and scary; known to be vicious toward males of any kind, this mullet will kill you if you piss her off. Training and socialization do not eliminate the natural-born aggression in these creatures. In many parts of the country their numbers are regulated because they are so feared. Most insurance companies won't provide coverage to homes with a Dykemullet in residence. Dykemullets should never be handled by anyone but professionals. Examples of Dykemullets are Aileen Wuornos and Darlie Routier. Know what they have in common besides their Dykemullets? That's right. They're both on death row (well, Aileen was until she was executed).

The Emoullet: Worn by self-cutting emo kids (melodramatic, depressed teenagers who write bad, whiny poetry, wear girl pants, act glum, and cry in the dark), this delicate mullet always features long bangs brushed over one eye (usually the right eye) with short (sometimes back-combed) hair in the back. It is commonly described as a "reverse mullet." They can be found at any open poetry reading or emo band concert.

The Femullet: This mullet appears on females and is often confused with the angrier, more dangerous Dykemullet. Femullets are generally easygoing, sporty, and paradoxically, either very quiet and docile or very loud and boisterous. Famous Femullets are tennis legend Billie Jean King, rock stars Pat Benatar and Joan Jett, Brady Bunch mom Florence Henderson, and Ashlee Simpson.

The Fohawk: Also "Fauxhawk," this style is a mutation of the familiar Mohawk. It is made without buzzing or shaving the sides of the head; it looks like a Mohawk when it is spiked with gel or spray, but unlike the Mohawk's shaved-to-the-skin sides (think Travis Bickle in *Taxi Driver*, or Mr. T), the Fohawk keeps the sides a bit longer so it can be worn down as well. Mullet professionals consider the Fohawk to be a hybrid cousin to the mullet. Famous Fohawks include Ryan Seacrest, host of *American Idol,* British soccer star David Beckham, and Bruno the Gay Austrian Fashion reporter from *Da Ali G Show.*

The Gullet: Inspired by the eighties band Flock of Seagulls (and in particular lead singer and former hairstylist Mike Score), this glorious mullet's identifying characteristic is the sweeping wings that make the head look like it is poised to take flight. This style depends heavily upon generous application of gel or hairspray to get the seagull wing effect. To emphasize the wings, the hair on the top of the head is sometimes allowed to grow long and then combed forward to resemble the seagull's beak. Mike Score discovered this breathtaking mullet, and he and his band are forever revered by Gulletheads everywhere.

The Jhericurullet: a mulletized version of the Jheri Curl, a hairstyle that was common and popular in the African American community in the late 1970s and throughout the '80s. This mullet works best on hair that is naturally tightly curled, like the Afro or the Jewfro; it is not recommended for beginners due to its high-maintenance upkeep. The Jhericurullet must be oiled to excess or it will die of dehydration. To help you remember its specialized care, memorize the following: "Here's a tip: it must drip." This style was worn by Little Richard, Michael Jackson (whose head burst into flames because of the excess oil and open flames during that infamous Pepsi commercial), Lionel Richie, Barry White, Pedro Martinez, and Jean Claude Van Damme.

The Mulletadon: Mainly seen on the heads of professional wrestlers, cage fighters, gladiators, and other alpha men, this pelt is often curly or wavy and is always long and flowing. Examples are Conan the Barbarian (Arnold's version) and any professional wrestler.

The Mullatino: Hispanics have done more for the mullet than just about any other group of people save white Southern males. Because of the natural full-bodied thickness of the Mullatino, these beautiful specimens can be shaped and sculpted into glorious monuments of mulletude that can be breathtaking to behold. Famous Mullatinos are Antonio Banderas, Fernando Lamas, Lorenzo Lamas, and Keith Hernandez.

The Mullitia: Worn by female military personnel, female law enforcement officers, and female astronauts, this mullet is known to be brave, loyal, and hardworking.

The Pullet: Sometimes called a Rooster, this mullet is often seen in the company of rock-and-roll stars. Its main feature is its spiky crown that resembles the feathers of a proud cock. Some famous pullets are Rod Stewart, Keith Richards, Ron Wood, and Iggy Pop.

The Skullet: This version has been popularized by American hero Benjamin Franklin and more recently professional wrestler Hulk Hogan and porn superstar Ron Jeremy. This mullet features a bald or shaved crown ringed with cascading hair on the sides and back.

T he term "Mullethead" was believed to have originated from the 1967 prison film *Cool Hand Luke,* starring Paul Newman and George Kennedy, in which Kennedy's character refers to Southern men with long hair as "Mullet Heads."

THE FIVE MEXICAN GENERALS PLAN

The politicians talk and talk about immigration, but in Austin and in Washington, they do absolutely nothing. Why is that? It's greed and politics, folks. Poly-ticks. Long before I offered the KISSP (Keep It Simple Stupid Politicians) program featuring ten thousand National Guard troops on the border; taxpayer ID cards for foreigners who want to work here, after criminal background checks; and socking it to employers big-time who hire illegals without the new ID cards; I voiced another suggestion to help stem illegal immigration. This was given to me by legendary Texas Ranger Joaquin Jackson. It was called "The Five Mexican Generals Plan." The people laughed when I first sat down at the piano to tell them about The Five Mexican Generals Plan. They're not laughing now.

They realize that no fundamental change in immigration policy is going to be introduced out of Austin or Washington, no matter who's in charge. The fact that the Democrats are now running things in the nation's capitol merely means that a different swarm of locusts and lobbyists has now descended upon the city. For their own personal, precious, political reasons, nothing will be delivered. I hope I am wrong, but common sense tells me that I'm right.

Therefore, just for the record, let me set down for you the plan Joaquin suggested to me, the plan that everybody thought was a joke but now is not so sure. The Five Mexican Generals Plan goes like this: We divide the border into five jurisdictions and we appoint a Mexican general in charge of each. Then we place a million dollars (or two million, whatever it takes) in a bank account, which we hold for each general. Then, every time we catch an illegal coming through his section, we withdraw ten thousand dollars. This will effectively shut off illegal immigration into Texas.

In 2006, George Bush Sr., the former president, invited me to Texas A&M to hear John McCain speak. Afterward, I got a chance to hang out a little with 41 and John McCain. I told them the Five Mexican Generals Plan. The former president chuckled over the plan quite a bit, but Senator McCain's response was quite different. He gave me a sort of wistful smile, then he said, "You know, that Five Mexican Generals Plan is probably better than anything we've got out there right now."

John McCain, of course, was right. It doesn't matter whether or not it's a joke, it merely points out that whatever we're doing (or not doing) now is not working. The plan may be a joke to some, but it's also common sense, the common sense of a man who knows the border and its problems more than most, Joaquin Jackson. Personally, I still strongly advocate the plan. I believe, along with a growing number of others, both inside and outside of government, that it's crazy enough to work.

Finally, let me just say that common sense is nothing new in government; it's merely something rare. Thomas Paine, one of the greatest, most significant Americans who ever lived, titled his pamphlet *Common Sense*. On his deathbed, Paine was harassed by clergymen demanding to know his nationality and his religion. Thomas Paine's only response was, "The world is my country; to do good is my religion."

In these troubled times, that's still a damn good answer.

BRING HIM ON

———————•———————

I'm pals with Clinton and pals with Bush—so, obviously, if John Kerry wants to be president, he has to make friends with me. Hey, is that my phone ringing?

"Start talkin'," I said as I picked up the blower.

"Kinkster," said a familiar voice, "this is John Kerry. I haven't been very happy with you lately."

"Why the long face, John?"

"Are you aware that I'm running for president of the United States?"

"Are you aware," I said somewhat indignantly, "that my books have been translated into more languages than your wife speaks?"

There was silence, followed by a peculiar choking sound. I

puffed patiently on my cigar and waited. One of the drawbacks to the telephone is that there's very little you can do to physically help the party on the other end of the line. Either Kerry would recover by himself or else he was definitely going to lose Ohio.

"I went to Vietnam," he said at last.

"I heard something about that," I said.

Indeed, it was one of the things I really liked about Kerry. America was full of patriotic-seeming people, from John Wayne to most of our top elected officials, who, when the time had come to serve their country, had not answered the call.

"I went to Vietnam myself earlier this year," I said. "Nobody told me the war was over." I heard what sounded like a practiced, good-natured chuckle from John Kerry. That was the trouble with politicians, I thought. Once they'd been on the circuit for a while, their words, gestures, even laughter—all were suspect, relegated to rote and habit. Something as natural as a smile became a mere rictus of power and greed. They couldn't help themselves; it was the way of their people. As Henry Kissinger once observed, "Ninety percent of politicians give the other ten percent a bad name."

"I'll get to the point," Kerry said. "I know you're pals with George W.—"

"I'm also pals with Bill Clinton," I said. "In fact, I'm proud to say I'm the only man who's slept with two presidents."

"That is something to be proud of. But I don't understand how you can support Bush's policies. I'm told you grew up a Democrat. What happened?"

What did happen, I wondered, to the little boy who cried

when Adlai Stevenson lost? What happened to the young man whose heroes were Abraham, Martin, and John? Time changes the river, I suppose, and it changes all of us as well. I was tired of Sudan being on the Human Rights Commission of the United Nations. I was tired of dictators with Swiss bank accounts, like Castro and Arafat and Mugabe, masquerading as men of the people. I was tired of Europeans picking on cowboys, everybody picking on the Jews, and the whole supposedly civilized world of gutless wonders, including the dinosaur graveyard called Berkeley, picking on America and Israel. As I write this, 1.2 million black Christian and Muslim Sudanese are starving to death, thanks to the Arab government in Khartoum and the worldwide mafia of France, Germany, China, Russia, and practically every Islamic country on the face of the earth. What happened to the little boy who cried when Adlai Stevenson lost? He died in Darfur.

"I don't know what happened," I said. "But as Joseph Heller once wrote, 'Something happened.'"

"You'll be back," said Kerry. "You'll be back."

He was telling me about his new health plan and how the economy was losing jobs when I heard a beeping sound on the blower and realized I had incoming wounded.

"Hold the weddin', John," I said. Then I pushed the call-waiting button.

"Start talkin'," I said.

"Hey, Kinkster!" said a familiar voice, this time with a big, friendly Texas drawl. "It's George W. How're things goin' at the ranch?"

"Fair to Midland, George," I said. "John Kerry's on the other line telling me about his new health plan. What's your health plan?"

"Don't get sick," said George with his own practiced, good-natured chuckle.

"He also told me the economy is losing jobs."

"What do you care, Kink? You told me you never had a job in your life."

"That's not true," I said. "I used to write a column for *Texas Monthly,* but it got outsourced to Pakistan."

"Kink, the economy's doin' fine. The country's turnin' the corner. We even have bin Laden in custody."

"I remember you told me that. Where is he now?"

"Time-share condominium in Port Aransas. His time's gonna run out two weeks before the election."

I chatted with George a while longer, then finished up with John. I had just returned to my chair and unmuted Fox News when the phone rang again. I power-walked into the office and picked up the blower.

"Start talkin'," I said.

"Kinky, it's Bill Clinton. How's it hangin', brother?"

"Okay, Bill. I just talked to George Bush and John Kerry on the phone."

"Skull and Bones! Skull and Bones! Tyin' up the telephones!" he chanted. "Hell, I still think about that night in Australia when you and me and Will Smith all went to that Maynard Ferguson concert. Too bad Will didn't bring his wife, wasn't it? Man, that was a party!"

I remembered that night, too. Millions of people undoubtedly love Bill Clinton, but I've always believed he has few real friends. That night he and I had talked about the recent death of one of his very closest, Buddy the dog. Like they say, if you want a friend in Washington, get a dog.

"Hey, Kink. There's a big ol' white pigeon sittin' on my windowsill here at my office in Harlem. Do you recall once asking me why there were white pigeons in Hawaii and dark pigeons in New York?"

"Sure. And you answered, 'Because God seeks balance in all things.'"

"That's right. Hell, I always wanted to be a black Baptist preacher when I grew up."

"Be careful what you wish for."

"Imagine, a white pigeon right in the middle of Harlem. If the whole world could see that, what do you reckon they'd say?"

"There goes the neighborhood?"

There followed the raw, real laughter of a lonely man who'd flown a little too close to the sun.

"Just remember, Kink," said Bill. "Two big bestselling authors like us got to stick together. Those other guys? Hell, they're only runnin' for president."

EPILOGUE

On January 4, 1993, the cat in this book and the books that preceded it was put to sleep in Kerrville, Texas, by Dr. W. H. Hoegemeyer and myself. Cuddles was fourteen years old, a respectable age. She was as close to me as any human being I have ever known.

Cuddles and I spent many years together, both in New York, where I first found her as a little kitten on the street in Chinatown, and later on the ranch in Texas. She was always with me, on the table, on the bed, by the fireplace, beside the typewriter, on top of my suitcase when I returned from a trip.

I dug Cuddles' grave with a silver spade, in the little garden by the stream behind the old green trailer where both of us lived in the summertime. Her burial shroud was my old New

York sweatshirt, and in the grave with her is a can of tuna and a cigar.

A few days ago I received a sympathy note from Bill Hoegemeyer, the veterinarian. It opened with a verse by Irving Townsend: "We who choose to surround ourselves with lives even more temporary than our own live within a fragile circle."

Now, as I write this, on a gray winter day by the fireside, I can almost feel her light tread, moving from my head and my heart down through my fingertips to the keys of the typewriter. People may surprise you with unexpected kindness. Dogs have a depth of loyalty that often we seem unworthy of. But the love of a cat is a blessing, a privilege in this world.

They say when you die and go to heaven all the dogs and cats you've ever had in your life come running to meet you.

Until that day, rest in peace, Cuddles.

STRANGE BEDFELLOWS

I sleep in an old ranch house in the Hill Country with a shot-gun under my bed and a cat on my head. The cat's name is Lady Argyle, and she used to belong to my mother before Mom stepped on a rainbow. It is not a pleasant situation when you have a cat who insists on sleeping on your head like a hat and putting her whiskers in your left nostril all night long at intervals of about twenty-seven minutes. I haven't actually timed this behavioral pattern, but it wouldn't surprise me if the intervals were precisely twenty-seven minutes. This precarious set of affairs could have easily resulted in a hostage situation or a suicide pact, but as of this writing, neither has occurred. The two reasons are because I love Lady as much as a man is capable of loving a cat, and Lady loves me as much as a cat is capable of loving a man. It is a blessing when an independent spirit like a cat loves you, and it's a common human failing to underestimate or trivialize such a bond. On the other hand, it's not a healthy thing to observe a man going to bed with a cat on his head like a hat. And, in the case of Lady and myself, there *are* observers.

The observers of this van Gogh mental hospital scenario are four dogs, all of whom despise Lady—though not half as much as Lady despises them. The dogs sleep on the bed, too, and they find it unnerving, not to say unpleasant, to be in the presence of a man who has a cat on his head. I've tried to discuss this with them on innumerable occasions, but it isn't easy to state your case to four dogs who are looking at you with pity in their eyes.

Mr. Magoo is five years old and highly skilled at how to be resigned to a sorry situation. He's a deadbeat dad, so his two sons, Brownie and Chumley, are with us as well. Brownie and Chumley were so named after my sister Marcie's two imaginary childhood friends and fairly recently have been left in my care, as she departed for Vietnam with the International Red Cross, an assignment she correctly deduced might be harmful to the health, education, and welfare of Brownie and Chumley. The animals divide their time between my place and the Utopia Animal Rescue Ranch, a sanctuary for abused and stray animals. (It's run by Nancy Parker and Tony Simons; my role is the Gandhilike figure. For more information go to utopiarescue.com).

If you've been spiritually deprived as a child and are not an animal lover, you may already be in a coma from reading this. That's good because I don't care a flea about people who don't love animals. I shall continue my impassioned tale, and I shall not stop until the last dog is sleeping.

The last dog is Hank. He looks like one of the flying monkeys in *The Wizard of Oz,* and he doesn't understand that the cat can and will hurt him and me and the entire Polish Army if we get in her way. Lady is about eighteen years old and has lived in this house on this ranch almost all her life, and she doesn't need to be growled at by a little dog with a death wish.

So I've got the cat hanging down over one side of my face like a purring stalactite with her whiskers poking into my left nostril and Hank on the other side who completely fails to grasp the mortal danger he's placing both of us in by playfully provoking the cat. It's 3:09 in the morning, and suddenly a deafening cacophony of barking, hissing, and shrieking erupts, with Lady taking a murderous swat at Hank directly across my fluttering eyelids and Mr. Magoo stepping heavily on my slumbering scrotum as all of the animals bolt off the bed simultaneously. This invariably signals the arrival of Dilly, my pet armadillo.

Dilly has been showing up with the punctuality of a German train in my backyard for years. I feed him cat food, dog food, bacon grease, anything. He is a shy, crepuscular, oddly Christlike creature whose arrival brings a measure of comfort to me at the same time it causes all of the dogs to go into attack mode. It is not really necessary to describe what effect this always has on Lady.

After I've slipped outside and fed Dilly, I gather the animals about me like little pieces of my soul. I explain to them once

again that Dilly is an old, spiritual friend of mine who is cursed with living in a state full of loud, brash Texans, and we don't have to make things worse. Somewhere there is a planet, I tell them, paraphrasing the great John D. MacDonald, inhabited principally by sentient armadillos who occasionally carve up dead humans and sell them as baskets by the roadside. Perhaps not surprisingly, the animals seem to relate to this peculiar vision. Then we all go back to bed and dream of fields full of slow-moving rabbits and mice and cowboys and Indians and imaginary childhood friends and tail fins on Cadillacs and girls in the summertime and everything else that time has taken away.

I DON'T

My fairy godmother, Edythe Kruger Friedman, is always telling me I should get married. As the survivor of two happy marriages—the last one to my father—she believes that a man and a woman living together in marital bliss is the only way to find true contentment in life. I believe in a neck without a pain.

Edythe feels so strongly about the importance of marriage and I feel so strongly about the importance of the freedom to wander in the raw poetry of time that often, when I go to her house for breakfast, we get into contentious little arguments on the subject. The debate sometimes becomes so heated that, if you happened to be listening from another room, you might assume that we were married. We are not, of course. I'll never be married. In fact, whenever I'm in Hawaii or Las Vegas or someplace where I happen to pass by a wedding in progress, I never fail to shout, "Stop before it's too late!"

It's already too late for me. I tell this to Edythe, but she never listens. I explain to her that I'm too old and set in my ways. I'm fifty-eight, though I read at the sixty-year-old level. And just because I'm fifty-eight and I've never been married, I tell her, does not mean I'm gay. It's only one red flag.

But don't you ever want to have a family? Edythe asks, pronouncing the word "family" with a soft reverence, as if it's the most wonderful state of being in the world. Have you ever seen *American Beauty*? I ask her. Families are only acquisition-mergers to create more and more of what there's already more than enough of as it is. It's just a rather narrow, selfish way of creating many little Edythes and many little Kinkys running around taking Ritalin and Prozac, playing video games, saying "awesome," sucking out all the money, energy, and time from your adult life, and growing up with an ever-increasing possibility of becoming the Unabomber. No thanks.

What I don't tell Edythe is that I already have a family. I have four dogs, four women, and four editors. This may seem like an unconventional arrangement to most people, but it does have at least one advantage over a traditional family. I don't have to find schools for them.

Speaking of school-age kids, another thing I don't tell Edythe is that I'm not really in the market for a fifty-eight-year-old belly dancer. I find myself going out with younger and younger women, most of whom happen to be from Dallas and can't remember where they were when JFK was assassinated, because they weren't born yet. Some of them, in fact, would not be born until several decades later, and they think JFK is an airport, RFK is a stadium, and Martin Luther King is a street running through their town.

"What could you two possibly have to talk about?" my fellow senior citizens often ask. It's true that the only time we ever find common ground is on her futon. She's never heard of Jack Benny, Humphrey Bogart, or Abbie Hoffman, and she thinks Hitler may have been a punk band in the early eighties. We get along fairly well, because I don't remember much, either.

There are two kinds of people in this world, I've always believed. I'm the kind who wants to sleep late and belch loudly and sometimes quite humorously at dinner parties. There are times, undoubtedly, when I feel alone, but I've found that it's always better to feel alone alone than to have that empty, soul-destroying feeling of feeling alone with somebody else. True happiness, I often tell people, must come from within. People don't always like to hear me espouse this great wisdom, but they do seem to prefer it to my belching at dinner parties.

The other kind of person, the polar opposite of myself, is what I like to call the marrying kind. I have three friends who, between them, have been married a dozen times, and I'm betting they're not through yet. Their names are Willie Nelson, Robert Duvall, and Billy Bob Thornton. All three tell me that they still believe in the institution of marriage, especially if it doesn't drive them to the mental institution. I think we're all probably creatures of habit, and the three of them just like being married. Or, possibly, after a failed marriage, the cowboy in them wants to get on that horse again to show he can still ride. A shrink might say they are repetitive neurotics. A shrink might also say that I have a fear of commitment. I would, of course, tell the shrink that I don't have a fear of commitment. I'm just afraid that someday my future ex-wife might not understand me. Then I would tell the shrink I want my money back.

Edythe, however, is oblivious to my protestations and my intransigence. She has a way of approaching the subject from many angles. Don't you ever want to be happy? she sometimes asks. No, I tell her. I don't want to be happy. Happiness is a highly perishable and transitory state, and it doesn't have a balanced export arrangement from one person to another, not to mention

CALLAHAN

that the import tax is too high. Besides, I'm concerned that happiness may have a negative effect on my writing.

Maybe you could write about meeting a nice Jewish girl, my fairy godmother suggests. I've met a lot of nice Jewish girls, I tell her, and they all seem to me to be culturally deprived. They all grew up in this country, yet most of them appear to have never heard the three words that Americans have come to live by.

"I love you?" asks Edythe.

"No," I tell her. "Attention, Wal-Mart shoppers."

Edythe usually continues nattering on until she finally broadsides me with her famous "right person" ploy. Maybe you just haven't found the right person yet, she says. I don't mention it, but I've already found the right person. Unfortunately, she was Miss Fire Ant, 1967. Things went downhill from there, both of us got our feelers hurt, and she wound up putting the bite on me.

The conversation usually concludes with Edythe employing what I call the "true love gambit." Don't I believe in true love? Haven't I ever been in true love? Of course I believe in it, I tell her. I've been in true love many times. I just try to avoid it as much as possible. For if there's one thing I know about true love, it is that sooner or later, it results in a hostage situation. Don't get me wrong: I'm not against marriage. I'm against my marriage. Anyway, I'm rather busy now. It's time to let the dogs in and the editors out. As for the women, that really isn't necessary. They have their own inexorable methods of working their way into your heart.

ZERO TO SIXTY

Soon I'll be sixty years old. Impossible, you say? How the hell do you think I feel? I don't know whether to have a birthday party or a suicide watch. I have received a few misguided cards and several inquiries from paleontologists, but basically, all being sixty really means is that you're old enough to sleep alone. In my case, having breezed through my entire adult life in a state of total arrested development, it's especially hard to realize that Annette Funicello is gone. I don't mean to make light of Annette Funicello. She died a tragic, lingering death, I believe, or maybe she's still with us, merely eclipsed by yet another former Mouseketeer, Britney Spears. The older and wiser I get, indeed, the less it is that I seem to know. Soon I may become such a font of wisdom and experience that I will know absolutely nothing at all. There are some, no doubt, who believe this stage of evolution has already occurred.

But this is where seniority comes to the rescue. For the older you get, the less you care what others may think of you. You may find yourself peeing in Morse Code, but you're still happy to share your wisdom and advice with the world. When hotel magnate Conrad Hilton was a very old man, someone asked him what was the most important thing he'd learned in life. "Always keep the shower curtain inside the tub," he answered. These may not sound like words to live by but, you'll have to admit, it does make for good practical advice. What's more important, of course, is all the water under the bridge that Hilton, for his own reasons, deliberately left out of the tub.

Possibly, even more importantly, I was cooking chicken gizzards for the dogs yesterday while watching *Wuthering Heights*. I forgot about the chicken gizzards until I saw smoke billowing out of the kitchen like the fog on the moors. This is what it amounts to, I told myself. To ask in the same breath, "Where are all our Heathcliffs? Where are all our Stellas?" And then, "Now what did I do with that damn coffee cup?" We usually find the coffee cup. But for everything else we've lost it's probably best simply to look back at life with a wistful smile and see it all as reflections in a carnival mirror.

According to my friend Dylan Ferrero, guys our age are in the seventh-inning stretch. This sports analogy may be lost in the lights by Iranian mullahs, adult stamp collectors, and other non–baseball fans. Or perhaps everybody knows what the seventh-inning stretch implies, but most of the world is too young or too busy to take the time to think about what it means to baseball or to life. A lot of wonderful things can happen after the seventh-inning stretch, of course, but, statistically speaking, it's pretty damn late in the game. None of us are getting younger or smarter. About all we can hope for is wise or lucky. But at least we're old enough to realize and young enough to know that when the Lord closes the door he opens a little window. Old age is definitely not for sissies, but those of us who are chronologically challenged may take comfort in the words of my favorite Irish toast: "May the best of the past be the worst of the future."

Sometimes I wonder why, God willing, I will likely make it to sixty when almost all the people I've loved are either dead or at the very least wishing they were. My fate, apparently, in the words of Winston Churchill, is to "keep buggering on." It's too late for me now to drive a car into a tree in high school. Yet I remain a late-blooming serious, a veteran soul for whom anything is possible, a man who at times feels like he is eighty, at times forty, and at times, a rather precocious twelve. What I do not feel is sixty. Sixty is ridiculous. Sixty is unthinkable. What God would send you to a Pat Green concert and send you home feeling like the Ancient Mariner? Hell, I've lived hard and loved hard and I was supposed to die young. If that had happened, of course, I never would have gotten the chance to order the Blue Plate for Senior Citizens at Luby's. And I probably wouldn't have noticed that John Wayne movies seem to be getting better and better.

All that notwithstanding, when you get to be a geezer you can gleefully gird yourself in garish geriatric garb. I've lately taken to wearing an oversized straw hat like the one van Gogh wore when he painted "Night Café." In van Gogh's case, unfortunately, he wore lighted candles on his hat, which was one reason they put him in the mental hospital. Other heroes of mine who wore large straw hats are Father Damien, Billy the Kid, and Don Quixote, none of whom saw sixty except for Quixote, who lives forever in the casino of fiction. And then, of course, there's always Juan Valdez.

My life, it seems, is a work of fiction, as well. As a reader, it's getting more and more difficult to find books that are older than I am. I'm currently reading, for instance, J. Frank Dobie's *A Texan in England*, which was written one year before I was born. When you read books created before you were, the ancient pages are green fuses, leaves of grass, through which, as if by some arcane form of spiritual osmosis, you seemingly receive the wisdom of the past. Writing at the ripe young age of sixty, however, is quite another matter. Larry McMurtry once remarked that nobody writes great fiction after the age of sixty. If this is true, I don't have long to find out. There was a time when my goals were to be fat, famous, financially fixed, and a *fagola* by fifty, but these lofty ambitions were never entirely achieved. Looking back, I realize that the goals themselves were not important. The only thing that was important was my being an alliterative asshole.

My father, in his later years, would wake up in the morning and say, "It almost feels good to be alive." The older I get, the more I understand how he felt. I have emulated Tom in surrounding myself with people still older than I, but needless to say, this task gets harder all the time. In the narrow, brittle world of material wealth I've tried to follow in my father's footsteps as well. When our accountant, Danny Powell, once asked my father what his financial goals were, Tom responded: "My financial goals are for my last check to bounce." This witty and wise outlook is very much in keeping with the gypsy's definition of a millionaire. The gypsies believe he is not a man with a million dollars, but a man who's *spent* a million dollars. The gypsies have been reading my mail. At sixty, I find that I am rich in the coin of the spirit. That may not buy you a cup of coffee these days, but it might just buy you a large, satisfying slice of peace of mind.

Finally, my incipient old age renders me the unalienable right to impart words of wisdom to all young little boogers whether they want to hear them or not. Some of the best I ever heard came from our old family friend Doc Phelps, one of my father's buddies in World War II, and for many years a biology professor at the University of Texas in Austin. Sometime in the midst of the eighties, on a trip to California, Tom and I stopped in to visit Doc one last time in a state hospital in New Mexico. Save us, Doc had almost no family or friends left, having been guilty of the mortal sin of outliving those who had once populated his life. We found him in a sterile room, void of even a shard of the personal possessions that would normally accrue to one who had lived such a rich and colorful life. Now he was dying in a little criblike hospital bed that very well may have resembled the crib in which he was born. It might've been easy to pity Doc, had he not given us something to take with us. "I'm a very lucky man," he said, "because I've loved many people in my life and I still do."

TENNIS ANYONE?

H aven't played tennis since high school. Haven't touched a racquet since Christ got aced, but I was pretty hot way back when. Got to the state finals in my senior year. My coach, Woodrow Sledge, always emphasized basic skills and ground strokes, a dominant serve, strong forehand and backhand, and a confident, yet conservative approach to the net. Therefore, he was never completely happy with what I will call the peculiar morality of my game. As long as I was winning, however, he'd just pat me on the back and shake his head.

They say sports does not build character, it just reveals it. Maybe this is true, but I think I learned important life lessons from the way I was able to win at tennis. To put the best face on it you could say I played like a high-stakes poker player or a riverboat gambler. There was nothing *wrong* with my game. It was just that I'd allowed my basic tennis fundamentals to be corrupted and seduced by weaving a web of artifice and delusion. Playing me was, for most good church-going Americans, like playing tennis with a sentient wall of carnival mirrors. And that has been my style ever since. Maybe even before I ever picked up a racquet.

You see, I was a chess prodigy when I was very young. At the tender age of seven I played the world grand master, Samuel Reschevsky, in Houston, Texas. He was there to play a simultaneous match with fifty people, all of whom, except for me, were adults. He beat all of us, of course, but afterward he told my dad he was sorry to have had to beat his son. He just had to be very careful with seven-year-olds. If he ever lost to one of them it'd be headlines.

The way you play a game, especially as a child, does more than reveal your character. I believe, after some grudging reflection, it provides a psychological peephole into the kind of person you will someday be. The way you play the game becomes an ingrained, living thing, a succubus that eventually determines how you play the game of life.

As far as chess was concerned, however, you could say I peaked at the age of seven. But by then, I now realize, I'd internalized the nature of the game. Very possibly, I'd unconsciously brought a sidecar of chess to my game of tennis. After all, tennis is not a team sport; the way you play tends to reveal who you really are. As long as you're winning, of course, nobody ever notices.

The game I played, the one that mildly irritated Coach Sledge, was an extremely duplicitous, downright deceitful at times, fabric of cat-and-mouse conceit. Yes, I'd begun with a strong, left-handed serve. But after that, things tended to degenerate. My stock-in-trade became a willful charade of evil fakes, feints, and last-moment, viciously undercut backhands. In other words, I was playing physical chess. There is no morality in chess or tennis, of course; morality, I suppose, is considered to be confined only to the game of life. Again, when you're winning, nobody notices.

Opposing players, many of whom were superior to me in basic tennis skills, were often left shaking their heads in what looked to me like a slightly more demonstrative impersonation of Coach Sledge. I would smile and graciously accept whatever accolades were thrown my way by any lookers-on. Sometimes there were stands full of people and sometimes there was only the sound of one hand clapping. It didn't matter. I knew. Deceiving the opponent was just as good as, indeed, it almost seemed preferable to, beating him with sound ground strokes and solid play. When you beat a highly skilled player in such a fashion, you almost have to struggle to contain your glee. I got pretty good at that, too.

When I graduated high school I left the sport of tennis far behind me, much as I'd done with chess back in my childhood. I could still play either of them, of course, but life was moving too fast for chess, and tennis seemed to require too high a degree of tedium in finding appropriate courts, lining up appropriate opponents, and constantly changing into appropriate clothing. It just didn't seem appropriate. Besides, I had college to deal with. My tennis racquet remained in the closet; the only webs of deceit associated with it were now woven exclusively by highly industrious spiders.

But, to be sure, I was quite busy myself. College was a whole new ballgame, as they say. Many of the kids who were the stars of my high school senior class went directly to pumping gasoline. New facts emerged in college, and I discovered to my personal delight that I flourished in this new environment. A deft talent for obfuscation works wonders with any seemingly sophisticated social set. "What you do in this world," the great Sherlock Holmes once said, "is a matter of no consequence. The question is what you can make people think you have done." Like Sherlock, I somehow instinctively knew never to reveal my methods.

No matter what anybody tells you, relationships between men and women on this particular planet are anything but straightforward and forthright. A successful relationship is usually governed by forces ingrained from childhood that one or both parties often remain totally unaware of. One may be a born gold digger looking forever for a free ride. One may be a caregiver, always looking for a bird with a broken wing. It's not so important who the two people are: timing and *what* they are is usually what counts. That's how the game is played and won. Sometimes, however, the bird with the broken wing heals up and beats you to death with it.

I met my future ex-wife, Leila Marie, in anthropology class, on one of the rare occasions I attended. I cut a lot of classes and

(I hope you won't be disappointed) I also cribbed an exam now and then in the manner of Ted Kennedy at Harvard. After all, I was enrolled in a highly advanced liberal arts program at the time that was mainly distinguished by the fact that every student had some form or other of facial tic. Every student, that was, except Leila Marie.

Leila Marie was a perky brunette with flashing green eyes who helped me write my monograph for anthropology: *The Flathead Indians of Montana*. Even with Leila Marie's talented and efficient help, it soon became apparent that liberal arts was never intended to be my long suit. I didn't want to become some stuffy professor helping students learn about the Flathead Indians of Montana. If they were burning with intellectual desire to find out about the Flathead Indians, they could damn well go to Montana and study campfire shards. I needed a field that was more applicable to today's world. A field in which I could help others, but also help myself. Meanwhile, the only field of study I seemed to be identifying with was Leila Marie.

Not only did Leila Marie appear to have an infinite amount of income, but she was also very easy on the eyes and lips. On top of that, no pun intended, she seemed to be willing to do anything it took to see that I succeeded. As things transpired, it was going to take quite a bit. I had decided that I wanted to go to medical school. It was not going to be easy and it was not going to be cheap. That was where Leila Marie came in.

I was always pretty strong when it came to the old gray-matter department but I must confess I was not prepared for organic chemistry. Leila Marie had to practically walk me through that one. But somehow we managed. I came to rely upon her judgment, her hard work ethic, and, yes, her financial resources. But I worked hard, too. Leila just worked a little harder. She even took a waitress job on the side when medical school tuition loomed near. That meant a lot to me. Besides, I've always been a sucker for attractive waitresses.

I didn't get into the best medical school, but I did get into medical school and that's what counts. In medical school, the guy who comes in last in his class is still called Doctor. We had to move to the island of Grenada and Leila Marie was beginning to look a bit shopworn from working two jobs, but we looked to the future and somehow kept moving forward. I believed in myself and Leila Marie believed in me and sometimes that's all that keeps you going. Fortunately, I could stand the sight of blood. Otherwise, I would've had to go to law school.

Leila Marie and I got married about the time I realized I wasn't going to be a brain surgeon. As long as I finished medical school and got my internship I didn't really care what kind of doctor I'd become. Just as long as I didn't have to make house calls. You had to be sort of ruthless about the whole thing or otherwise you wouldn't get through. What was the point of saving the world if you couldn't save yourself? So I became a proctologist. It's nothing to be ashamed of, I figured. Besides, you have to work with so many assholes every day you might as well get paid for it.

After medical school we moved to a new town where I took my internship at the local hospital. If you've never gone through an internship you probably have no idea how much of your personal life it consumes. Every night in the emergency room I'd witness the flotsam and jetsam of humanity walk, crawl, wheel themselves, or be carried past my increasingly jaded irises. People with limbs missing. People with gunshot wounds. People stuck together fucking. It was a real mess but I think I can truly say that it made a doctor out of me. All those hours at the hospital, of course, had a rather debilitating effect on my marriage. But it was at about that time that I took a turn for the nurse.

She was a gorgeous, young, blue-eyed blonde from the Great Northwest and she had a real way with people and one of them was me. When you work with somebody in life-and-death situations, you really get to know them. Her name was Lana Lee and I credit her with bringing the fun and excitement back into my life. Somehow, I had grown past Leila Marie, who'd continued working her dreary jobs and complaining about the long hours the internship was causing me to keep. It was kind of sad, but increasingly Leila Marie seemed to be living in the past and I seemed to be living for the future. And Lana Lee seemed inexorably to be a part of that future.

If there's one thing I know about destiny it is that you can't count on it forever. I knew things couldn't go on like this, and sure enough they didn't. Tragically, in the first year of my private practice, Leila Marie died rather suddenly of a fairly ar-

cane illness that is faintly related in the literature to toxic shock syndrome. The malady was impossible to treat, diagnose, or detect, and it caused me no little grief to realize the irony that I was a doctor and there was nothing I could do for her. The subsequent autopsy revealed no clue as to the cause of her death.

Lana Lee was there to support me, however, and one thing led to another. When the Lord closes the door He opens a little window, they say. In my case, at least, it certainly seems that way. There was, indeed, a nasty little hint of suspicion surrounding me after Leila Marie's death, but it comes with the territory. Doctors have become as used to this sort of mean-minded gossip as we are to scribbling prescriptions or working with HMOs. I didn't let it get me down.

Today, I'm happily married to Lana Lee and I have a thriving practice. If you're patient and you see a lot of patients, the medical profession can provide a very lucrative lifestyle. Not only that, but it's a good way to help serve your fellow man. And speaking of serving, guess what? I've taken up tennis again.

SMOKE GETS IN YOUR EYES

When I was a child I spoke as a child and, believe it or not, I smoked as a child. At the tender age of eighteen months, when my mother's back was turned, a prescient if somewhat perverse uncle surreptitiously substituted a cigar for my pacifier. Don't know if I should thank Uncle Eli or not but sixty-one-and-a-half years later I'm not only still smoking, but I've started my own cigar company. I named it Kinky Friedman Cigars or, as it's become increasingly and affectionately known throughout Texas and the world, KFC.

Though smoking in general is currently being attacked from all quarters, I have no qualms about becoming the George Foreman for my product. I strongly believe smoking cigars can yield at least three positive effects—reducing stress, increasing longevity, and irritating the hall monitors. From time to time, of course, as the situation dictates, I still resort to the pacifier. This draws the occasional rude comment one might expect but truthfully there's not that much difference between a good cigar and the time-honored pacifier. After a liftetime of smoking I only have one or two taste buds left. But I can assure you, those little buds are having one hell of a party.

Simply to suck on a cigar these days is practically tantamount to making a political statement. Politicians and bureaucrats at all levels of government have failed so disastrously at resolving the issues that matter to most people, i.e. health care, education, immigration, political reform, energy costs, property taxes, utility bills, criminal justice issues, environment, toll roads, etc., that all they seem able to do is tax tobacco and pass ever-more-stringent smoking regulations. In other words, the combined might of our government appears only capable of criminalizing trivia. You'd think George Washington crossed the Delaware expressly to keep Kinky Friedman and his cigar at least twenty feet away from the entrance to Katz's Deli.

As founder of Kinky Friedman Cigars, I am, of course, well aware of some people's concerns regarding the use of our product. But more laws and more regulations are not the answer. Folks, we're turning our beautiful country into nothing more than a condo association. Rules, regulations, and political correctness are strangling the best thing America has to offer— freedom. Freedom of speech, freedom of expression, freedom to be who you are. If you own a bar and want to have smoking, you should be able to put a sign on the door, "Smoking allowed."

If you don't want smoking, you put up a sign, "No smoking." Maybe you have a bar and you don't want drinking. That's fine, too. If you're gay, you can go to a gay bar; if you're straight, you can go to the Jewish Singles Purim Party. This is the way America should be.

Instead, we have a Houston city councilman explaining why he voted for a city-wide ban on smoking in bars. "What if I want to bring my kids to the bar?" he said. Common sense is up in smoke, folks. Meanwhile, misguided zealots behind draconian smoking regulations quite often fall back on the argument that, "It's for your health." They haven't noticed, apparently, that whenever you see a ninety-year-old geezer, most of the time he's still puffing a stogie. On the other hand, you almost never see a ninety-year-old smoking a cigarette. This is because we cigar smokers religiously follow the wise example of Bill Clinton. We don't inhale. That's why my message to young people is, "Cigarette bad—cigar good."

Unfortunately, not everybody's fired up—no pun intended—about my new venture. For example, one person recently contacted the Web site with the following message: "It is sad to see an icon turn into a whore."

"I don't care what you call me," I wrote back. "Rick Perry calls himself a public servant. Al Sharpton calls himself a civil rights leader. Besides, whores usually tend to hang around with a better class of people than icons." I am waiting, with bated smoke-rings, for his response.

The other folks who aren't too happy with Kinky Friedman Cigars are some of the big cigar industry Goliaths who don't like seeing little Davids sharing their shelf-space in Texas stores. Nevertheless, after only a matter of months as a small, start-up company, my friend and now CEO, Little Jewford (He's a Jew and he drives a Ford), has filed the following report: "We've moved more than 100,000 sticks in the last quarter. You're on track to become the Famous Amos of the cigar world!"

While being the face of the company seems like fun, I knew we still needed some brains. For that, I tapped a true cigar professional, Sean Robinson, to be president of KFC. Sean traveled to the jungles of Honduras and there, amidst machine guns, tarantulas, and beautiful women rolling beautiful cigars on their beautiful thighs, he befriended a man named Nestor, the king of the Cuban cigar-makers, who promised to create a special new blend for Kinky Friedman Cigars.

When Sean returned, he had several small darts in his back, compliments of the Mosquito Indians, and five new lines of cigars—The Governor, The Kinkycristo, The Texas Jewboy, The Willie (which has a little twist on one end), and The Utopian, the only cigar in America benefiting animal rescue. Profits go to Utopia Animal Rescue Ranch. You can get all these cigars at good cigar stores everywhere or you can order sample packs and boxes right off the Web site, kinkycigars.com.

What else do you guys have to offer? you may be wondering. Well, I'll share a little trade secret with you. Sean, Nestor, and Gary Irvin, our chief tobacconist, are currently developing three new lines: The Clinton, a replica of the Cuban Montecristo I once presented to Bill at the White House; The Kinky

Lady, with the butt (of the cigar, that is) dipped in honey; and a brand new cigar, the blend of which, I am told, enhances the flavor of tequila.

Now I'm sure there are those who will be casting asparagus upon the Kinkster, but I promise you my words are not hazardous to anybody's health. I'm just saying that God's not going to honk your horn until He's good and ready. So you might as well find what you like and let it kill you.

Now don't get me wrong. I admire Lance Armstrong and his work fighting cancer, and I consider him a friend. I respect anyone with sincere and genuine intentions regarding the welfare of all people. What I object to are these officious little boogers who use health as a smoke screen to empower their agenda and themselves. What I want these people to put in their pipes and smoke is this: Spain, Portugal, Israel, Japan, Korea, Italy, France, and Greece all have more smokers per capita than the U.S. They also have lower rates of lung cancer and heart disease. What can we conclude from this? Speaking English is killing us!

PART II

MY PERSONAL
HEROES

THE NAVIGATOR

***

Because I'm the oldest living Jew in Texas who doesn't own real estate, and given my status in general as a colorful character, there are those who profess to be surprised that I ever, indeed, had a father or a mother. I assure you, I had both.

For many years my parents owned and directed Echo Hill Ranch, a summer camp near Kerrville where I grew up, or maybe just got older. I remember my dad, Tom Friedman, talking to all of the campers on Father's Day in the dining hall after lunch. Each summer he'd say essentially the same words: "For those of you who are lucky enough to have a father, now is the time to remember him and let him know that you love him. Write a letter home today." Many years have passed since I last heard Tom's message to the campers, but love, I suppose, has no "sell by" date.

When my father was a young boy growing up in the Chicago of the late twenties, his first job was working for a Polish peddler. The man had a horse and cart that was loaded up with fruits and vegetables, and Tom sat on the very top. Through the streets and alleys of the old West Side they'd go, with the peddler crying his wares in at least five languages and my father running the purchases up to the housewives who lived on the top floors of the tenement buildings. There were trolley cars then and colorful clotheslines strung across the sooty alleys like medieval banners. My father still remembers the word the peddler seemed to cry out more than any other. The word was *kartofel*. It is Polish for "potato."

In November 1944 my mother, Minnie, gave birth to me in a manger somewhere on the south side of Chicago. (I lived there one year, couldn't find work, and moved to Texas, where I haven't worked since.) And all this time my father was far away fighting for his country and his wife and a baby boy he might never see. Tom was a navigator in World War II, flying a heavy bomber for the Eighth Air Force, the old B-24, also known as the Liberator, which, in time, it was. Tom's plane was called the I've Had It. He flew thirty-five successful missions over Germany, the last occurring on November 9, 1944, two days after he'd learned that he was a brand-new father. As the navigator, the responsibility fell to him to bring the ten-man crew back safely. In retrospect, it's not terribly surprising that fate and the powers that be had selected Tom to be the navigator. He was the only one aboard the *I've Had It* who possessed a college degree. He was also the oldest man on the plane. He was twenty-three years old.

After each successful mission it was the custom to paint a small bomb on the side of the plane; in the rare instance of shooting down an enemy plane, a swastika was painted. When one incoming crew, however, accidentally hit a British runway maintenance worker, a small teacup was painted on the side of the plane, practically engendering an international incident.

Tom was a hero in what he still refers to as "the last good war." For his efforts, he received the Distinguished Flying Cross and the Air Medal with three Oak Leaf clusters and the heartfelt gratitude of his crew. Yet the commanding officer's first words to Tom and his young compatriots had not been wrong. The CO had told them to look at the man on their left and to look at the man on their right. "When you return," he'd said, "they will not be here." This dire prophecy proved to be almost correct. The Mighty Eighth suffered a grievous attrition rate during the height of the war.

After the war Tom and Min settled in Houston, where Tom pioneered community action programs, and Min became one of the first speech therapists in the Houston public schools. In the late fifties they moved to Austin, where Tom was a professor of educational psychology at the University of Texas. It was in 1953, however, that my parents made possibly their greatest contribution to children far and wide by opening Echo Hill Ranch. My mother passed away in 1985, but Tom, known as Uncle Tom to the kids, still runs the camp.

Like most true war heroes, Tom rarely talks about the war. My sister, Marcie, once saw Tom sitting alone in a darkened room and asked, "Is everything all right, Father?" To this Tom replied, "The last time everything was all right was August 14, 1945." That was the day Japan surrendered.

On a recent trip to O'Hare Airport in Chicago, I commandeered a limo and drove through the area where Tom had grown up. There were slums and suburbs and Starbucks, and the trolley cars and the clotheslines and the peddler with his horse and cart were gone. "Kartofel," I said to the limo driver, but he just looked straight ahead. Either he wasn't Polish or he didn't want any potatoes.

Today Tom lives in Austin with his new wife, Edythe Kruger, and his two dogs, Sam and Perky. He has three children and three grandchildren. He eats lunch at the Frisco and still plays tennis with his old pals. He did not, as he contends, teach me everything I know. Only almost everything. He taught me tennis. He taught me chess. He taught me how to belch. He taught me to always stand up for the underdog. He taught me the importance of treating children like adults and adults like children. He is a significant American because by his example, his spirit, and his unseen hand, he has guided children of all ages safely through the winding, often torturous courses of their lives. One of them was me.

Tom's war is long over. Indeed, the whole era seems gone like the crews who never came home, lost forever among the saltshaker stars. And yet, when the future may look its darkest, there sometimes occurs an oddly comforting moment when, with awkward grace, the shadow of a silver plane flies inexplicably close to my heart. One more mission for the navigator.

DON IMUS DIED
FOR OUR SINS

Because of the illness known as human nature, I suppose it was necessary for Don Imus to die for our sins. Every good Christian knows, however, that's already been done by Jesus. When judgment comes, they will tell you, it's not about the bad things you may have done; it's about the good things you do. Throwing stones in glass houses notwithstanding, there probably isn't a single one of Imus's vocal critics who comes anywhere close to matching his record of philanthropy or good acts on this earth.

Judge a man by the size of his enemies, my father used to say. If two neighbors are bickering over a fence line, that doesn't tell you much. But consider a man who year after year has raised countless millions of dollars for charity and has

fought hand-to-hand combat against childhood cancer, autism, and SIDS (none of which, by the way, have ever afflicted himself or his family), and well, you've got a rodeo clown who not only rescues the cowboy but saves the children as well. Imus's work has also been well documented in fighting relentlessly for the fallen, forgotten heroes of a rather dubiously conceived war.

But Imus's good works, which are a matter of record, as well as a matter of heart, will indubitably be judged by a higher authority—higher than the media, the racemongers, or the rats leaving the sinking ship. Imus sailed that ship for almost forty years as dangerously close to the truth as he could get. There are two kinds of sailors, they say: the sailor who fights the sea, and the sailor who loves the sea. Imus loved the sea. He also loved his job. He loved children and animals and yes, even people. I speak in the past tense only because Imus is gone for the moment. I predict he will be back, very possibly bigger than ever. Every saint was once a sinner and every sinner was once a saint.

I met Imus on the gangplank of Noah's Ark. He was then and remains today a truth-seeking missile with the best bullshit meter in the business. Far from being a bully, he was a spiritual chop-buster, never afraid to go after the big guys with nothing but the slingshot of ragged integrity. I watched him over the years as he struggled with his demons and conquered them. This was not surprising to me. Imus came from the Great Southwest, where the men are men and the emus are nervous. And he did it all with something that seems, indeed, to be a rather scarce commodity these days. A sense of humor.

There's no excusing Imus's recent ridiculous remark, but there's something not kosher in America when one guy gets a Grammy and one gets fired for the same line. The Matt Lauers and Al Rokers of this world live by the cue card and die by

CALLAHAN

the cue card; Imus is a rare bird, indeed—he works without a net. When you work without a net as long as Imus has, sometimes you make mistakes. Wavy Gravy says he salutes mistakes. They're what make us human, he claims. And humanity, beyond doubt, is what appears to be missing from this equation. If we've lost the ability to laugh at ourselves, to laugh at each other, to laugh together, then the PC world has succeeded in diminishing us all. Political correctness, a term first used by Josef Stalin, has trivialized, sanitized, and homogenized America, transforming us into a nation of chain establishments and chain people.

Take heart, Imus. You're merely joining a long and legendary laundry list of individuals who were summarily sacrificed in the name of society's sanctimonious soul: Socrates, Jesus, Galileo, Joan of Arc, Mozart, and Mark Twain, who was decried as a racist until the day he died for using the n-word rather prolifically in Huckleberry Finn. Today many people believe the book to be the greatest work of fiction in the western world because Twain created a slave named Jim who was a man of integrity, dignity, and humanity in a world full of scoundrels and hypocrites.

Speaking of which, there will always be plenty of Sharptons and Jacksons around. There will be plenty of cowardly executives; plenty of lazy, Gotcha! media types; plenty of fairweather friends; and plenty of Jehovah's Bystanders, people who believe in God but just don't want to get involved. In this crowd, it could be argued that we need a Don Imus just to wake us up once in a while.

Finally, I believe New York will miss its crazy cowboy and America will miss the voice of a free-thinking, independent-minded, rugged individualist. I believe MSNBC will lose many viewers and CBS radio, many listeners. Too bad for them. That's what happens when you get rid of the only guy you've got who knows how to ride, shoot straight, and tell the truth.

ANIMAL HEROES

Binti Jua: Binti Jua is a western lowland gorilla who resides in the Brookfield Zoo in Chicago, Illinois. Her aunt is Koko, the gorilla who is famous for her ability to communicate with humans using American Sign Language.

A three-year-old child climbed a railing at the Brookfield Zoo's gorilla exhibit and promptly fell eighteen feet down into the enclosure. The fall knocked the boy unconscious. Zookeepers rushed to rescue him, but his fall placed him in an area that they couldn't reach quickly. Binti, who witnessed the child's fall, rushed over to the unconscious boy and gently carried him in her arms to a safe area where zoo officials could treat him. Her own baby, Koola, clutched her back throughout the entire rescue. The little boy Binti Jua saved spent four days in the hospital and was then released. Binti Jua's quick reactions that day made her a hero.

Cher Ami: Messenger pigeons were used extensively during both world wars. In World War I, the U.S. Army Signal Corps used six hundred pigeons in France. One of their carrier pigeons, a Black Check cock called Cher Ami, was awarded the French "Croix de Guerre with Palm" for heroic service while delivering twelve important messages in Verdun. On his final mission in October 1918, he delivered a message despite having been shot. The crucial message, found in the capsule hanging from a ligament of his shattered leg, saved around two hundred U.S. soldiers of the 77th Infantry Division's "Lost Battalion" in the battle of the Argonne. He is enshrined in the Smithsonian Institution, and is currently on display in the National Museum of American History's "Price of Freedom" exhibit.

Paddy: On November 25, 1944, Royal Air Force war bird "Paddy" was decorated for his effort in the war against Nazi Germany. This brave bird made the fastest recorded crossing of the English Channel, delivering messages from Normandy for D-Day, traveling 230 miles in 4 hours, 5 minutes. When receiving his Order of Merit he was described as "exceptionally intelligent."

Lola: Lola the white rat is the top student in her class at a police school in Sibate, near Bogata. She is among six rats being trained to sniff out land mines in Colombia. Security experts credit the Revolutionary Armed Forces of Colombia (FARC), and the smaller National Liberation Army (ELN), with planting mines because they are effective in preventing soldiers and police from raiding their coca fields and the camps they use to hold thousands of kidnap victims. The International Campaign to Ban Land Mines estimates that 100 million mines have been laid worldwide, from antipersonnel and antitank mines hidden underground to above-ground mines triggered by tripwires. More than 1,075 Colombians were killed or maimed by stepping on mines in 2005, a higher number than in any other heavily mined country such as Cambodia or Afghanistan.

Colombian police animal trainers, frustrated by seeing so many of their valuable explosive-sniffing dogs blown up by stepping on mines planted by the leftist rebels, decided to explore other ways to locate and detonate the explosives. Inspired by a similar pilot program in Mozambique, Colombian police purchased six rats and were surprised to find that they learned to sniff out explosives, such as C4, twice as fast as dogs and, unlike even the best mine-detecting dog or human, they are relentlessly single-minded. Rats are plentiful, cheap, and easily transported. At about 220 grams each, Lola and her classmates are too light to detonate mines accidentally. "The dogs are heavy enough to set off the explosion, sometimes killing officers nearby," said Police Colonel Javier Cifuentes, head of the program at the National Police base in Sibate. "The rats can stand on a mine without anything happening."

Katrina: In March 2006, The Humane Society of the United States hosted the twentieth annual Genesis Awards, a program that honors works from the big screen, the small screen, and from print-media news and entertainment that convey the message of respect and compassion for animals. The guest of honor was Katrina, a black Labrador retriever who proved herself a hero in the aftermath of one of the deadliest hurricanes in the history of the United States.

On August 29, 2005, Hurricane Katrina's storm surge caused several breaches in levees around New Orleans, leaving 80 percent of the city submerged, tens of thousands of victims clinging to rooftops, and hundreds of thousands scattered to shelters around the country. Out of the devastation of Hurricane Katrina, many stories of heroism and bravery came to the forefront. One man's tale in particular captured the hearts of people worldwide. In an on-the-spot interview, the man described how, when the waters rose, a nameless black dog pulled him to higher ground and saved him from drowning. The dog stayed with him until he was later rescued by helicopter. Despite the man's pleas, the dog had to be left behind. Like many of Hurricane Katrina's animal victims, she would have been abandoned if it weren't for the actions of a television crew covering the big storm; the crew rescued the dog from the flood waters and promptly named her "Katrina." After an unsuccessful search for Katrina's owners, she was adopted by KCAL photographer Jeff Mailes and taken to her new home in California. Katrina was later featured in a two-part report on the hurricane in New Orleans.

Roselle and Salty: On September 11, 2001, guide dog Roselle successfully led her owner Michael Hingson to safety from the seventy-eighth floor of the North Tower, shortly before the World Trade Center collapsed. On that same day, Omar Eduardo Rivera was in his seventy-first floor office. After the first plane struck, Rivera heard glass breaking and he un-leashed his guide dog, hoping that the golden retriever would escape. But, as Rivera told Reuters, "The dog was very nervous, and he ran off but came back and kept by my side. He didn't bark." Instead, Salty led Rivera to an emergency exit and down the stairs.

Both Roselle and Salty led their owners to safety by picking their way through the buildings and down to the debris-filled streets. The guide dogs were honored for their bravery with the British Dickin Medal for their devotion to duty during the World Trade Center tragedy. The Dickin medal is recognized worldwide as "the animals' Victoria Cross"—in American terms, the animal equivalent of the Congressional Medal of Honor.

Staff Sergeant Reckless: Decorated equine war hero Staff Sergeant Reckless served in the second Battalion, fifth Regi-ment of the first Division of the United States Marine Corps in Korea during the Korean War. Reckless was purchased from a Korean boy who needed money to buy his sister an artificial leg, according to Marine Lieutenant Colonel Andrew Geer, commander of the unit. Geer wrote two articles about the horse for the *Saturday Evening Post* in the 1950s and later wrote a book entitled *Reckless, the Pride of the Marines*. Trained as an ammunitions carrier, the horse served at the bloody Battle of Vegas Outpost, March 28–30, 1953. In his book, Geer wrote: "Every yard she advanced was showered with explosives. Fifty-one times she marched through the fiery gauntlet of the Red barrage—and she saved the day for the Leathernecks." Marines who served with her remember seeing the horse hero walking around military camps in Korea wearing a blanket bearing stripes and her Purple Heart.

After the war ended, Reckless was left in South Korea as her fellow Marines returned to the States, but after publication of Geer's article, *Post* readers and friends of the horse arranged to bring her to the United States. In 1959, five years after arriving at Camp Pendleton, Reckless was promoted to a staff sergeant, according to a November 1992 article in *Leatherneck* magazine. The decorated war veteran passed away in 1968 and was survived by three offspring.

Judy: Judy, an English pointer, served on a Royal Navy vessel before and during World War II. She was known for pointing out the approach of hostile Japanese aircraft long before any of the human crew could hear them. When her ship was sunk in action and the crew became prisoners of war, Judy continued to perform her duties by helping find food and providing comfort and companionship to her fellow sailors. She was the only animal to have been officially registered as a Japanese prisoner of war.

After the war, Judy was adopted by Frank Williams and smuggled back to England. She was awarded the Dickin Medal in May 1946. Her citation reads: "For magnificent courage and endurance in Japanese prison camps, which helped to maintain morale among her fellow prisoners and also for saving many lives through her intelligence and watchfulness."

In 2006 her collar and medal went on display in the Imperial War Museum, London, as part of "The Animals' War" exhibition.

Scarlett: On March 30, 1996, a homeless mother cat and her five kittens were in an abandoned garage allegedly used as a crack house in Brooklyn, New York. A fire broke out in the building and Ladder Company 175 was called, and they quickly extinguished the blaze. One of the firefighters on the scene, David Giannelli, noticed the mother cat carrying her kittens away from the garage one by one. "What she did," he said, "was she ran in and out of that building five times, got them all out, and then started moving them one by one across the street." The cat, later nicknamed "Scarlett," had been severely injured in the process of pulling her kittens from the fire. Her eyes were blistered shut, her ears and paws were seriously burned, and the hair on her face was almost completely burned away. After saving the kittens, she touched each of them with her nose to make sure they were all there and alive, as the blisters on her eyes kept her from being able to see them. Satisfied that her kittens were safe, she then collapsed, unconscious.

Gianelli took Scarlett and her four-week-old kittens to the veterinary clinic of the North Shore Animal League in Port Washington, New York, where they were treated for their injuries. One kitten, weakened by smoke inhalation, died of a virus. After three months of treatment and recovery, Scarlett and her four surviving kittens were well enough to be adopted. The story of Scarlett's heroic efforts to save her babies resulted in worldwide publicity; the League received seven thousand letters from people offering to adopt them. A committee at the North Shore Animal League read the letters and picked three families. Two kittens, Oreo and Smokey, went to Debbie Palmarozzo of

Long Island. The two other kittens, Samsara and Panuki, who were inseparable during their recovery time at the clinic, were adopted by Corinne and Ginette Vercillo, also of Long Island. Scarlett was adopted by Karen Wellen.

The North Shore Animal League created the Scarlett Award for Animal Heroism in Scarlett's honor. This award is presented to animals who have engaged in heroic acts to benefit others, whether humans or animals.

"She's a wonderful, gentle animal who did a courageous thing," said NSAL shelter manager Marge Stein. "It shows with all creatures—animals or people—there's no way of measuring a mother's love."

TANGLED UP IN BOB

─────────●─────────

With the publication of Bob Dylan's long-awaited autobiography, *Chronicles* (Simon and Schuster), on the heels of a reissue of my old friend Larry "Ratso" Sloman's classic, *On the Road With Bob Dylan* (Three Rivers Press), I've got an excuse to tell you about the first time I met Bob. It was the fall of 1973, and my band, the Texas Jewboys, was playing the Troubadour in Los Angeles. One night Bob walked in barefoot, wearing a white robe. Possibly he thought he was Jesus Christ or Johnny Appleseed, or maybe he'd just gotten out of the bath, but everybody definitely treated him like a god. He was friendly, cryptic, and almost shy when he was introduced to us after the show. Later, we watched from the dressing room window as he got into his limo in the alley behind the club. Willie Fong Young, our bass player, said it best at the time: "He may not have any shoes, but at least he's got a limo."

It wasn't long after that that his road manager called my road manager (who, cosmically enough, was named Dylan Ferrero). I was instructed to go out on the Santa Monica pier at midnight and meet a baby-blue 1960 Cadillac convertible that would take me to Bob. After a long, mystical journey, I wound up at the home of Roger McGuinn, the founder of the Byrds, who was to become a friend of mine even though I did make the following comment to him that night: "There is a time to live and a time to die and a time to stop listening to albums by the Byrds."

By two o'clock in the morning, I had still not seen Bob, but I did stumble upon Kris Kristofferson talking to a young groupie he'd apparently just met. Kris looked up and said, "Kinky?" Simultaneously, the girl and I responded, "Yes." Kris pointed me in the direction of the kitchen. I wandered in, and there was Bob sitting on the counter, strumming a guitar and singing a song I'd written, "Ride 'em Jewboy."

It was fashionable in the early seventies to talk long into the night about "life and life only," and Bob and I did that. I told him about my recent trip with the members of Led Zeppelin aboard the Starship, their private jet with a fireplace, and that I was particularly excited about urinating backstage next to Jimmy Page. Bob was not impressed. "They have nothing to say," he said. "You and Kris have a lot to say. You should say it. Without," he went on, "using makeup and dry ice."

Later, I went off to find a drink, and when I returned, Roger was helping Bob up off the floor. "The wine's not agreeing with him," Roger said. That night, I suppose, I wasn't agreeing with him much either, but that could have been because I had a chip the size of Dallas on my shoulder. Or it could just be that time changes the river. However you look at it, it's now clear that Led Zep, like so many other acts, has been relegated to the bone orchard of nostalgia, while Bob remains a spiritual beacon in a world largely remarkable for its unwillingness to be led to the light.

Traveling and making music with Bob is a rare opportunity to see a magic messenger at work and play. In 1976 Bob asked me to join him and Joan Baez, Joni Mitchell, Eric Clapton, Ringo Starr, Allen Ginsberg, and many others as part of his Rolling Thunder Revue, which traveled across America that year, leaving behind some satisfied women, some wildly enthusiastic audiences, and some brain cells that promised they'd get back to us later.

I hung out a lot with Bob after that tour, and as mesmerizing and untouchable as he seems onstage, offstage he can be extremely warm and witty. Imagine Bob and me standing in the parking lot of a seedy motel in Fort Worth at two-thirty in the morning with a redneck motel manager repeatedly asking him for his driver's license. Or picture Bob at a barbecue at my parents' house in Northwest Austin. (When my mother brought him a plate, he said, "Thanks, Mrs. Friedman. You must be very proud of your son.") I remember shopping with Bob at the famous Nudie's in North Hollywood, where he saw a rhinestone jacket embroidered with Jesus' face. "A guy ordered this a long time ago," Nudie told Bob, "but he never came back for it." "He has now," said Bob. Bob bought the jacket, wore it for one performance, and then gave it to me. The Bob Dylan Jesus Jacket promptly brought me seven years of bad luck, after which I sold it at Sotheby's. (It hung for a while in the Hard Rock Cafe in Tel Aviv.) Several years ago I caught up with Bob in New York and told him what I'd done with the jacket. He shook his head and said, "Bad move."

Speaking of jackets, I once spent a month with Bob in the village of Yelapa, off the western coast of Mexico. Although it was over 100 degrees every day, Bob never took off his heavy leather jacket. I knew he was from Minnesota, but it did seem somewhat odd, so one day on the beach I asked him about it. His answer was to tell me a story about the king of the gypsies, and how, when the king got old, all his wives and children left him. I thought at the time that Bob might be feeling a chill that few of us ever feel.

People often ask me what Bob is really like. He's naturally shy and superstitious and hates to be photographed because he believes that every picture taken of him reduces his chances of becoming an Indian when he grows up. Bob, in fact, has a lot in common with the Native American people. They both believe, for instance, that you can't own land or a waterfall or a horse. The only thing they both believe you can own is a casino. Yet Bob's been so many things in his life that it's almost impossible to pin him down. He's been a vegetarian, an Orthodox Jew, a born-again Christian, a Buddhist, a poet, a pilgrim, a picker, a boxer, a biker, a hermit, a chess player, a beekeeper, and an adult stamp collector—and almost everything, except a Republican, that a human being can possibly be when a restless soul is forever evolving toward his childhood night-light.

And, of course, he's a very funny American. I remember once when we had to book a flight at the last minute and there was nothing in first class available. When we got back to coach, there were only a few seats left and Bob found, much to his dismay, that he was seated next to an enthusiastic young female fan. "I can't believe I'm sitting next to Bob Dylan!" she screamed. Bob gazed calmly at the girl. "Pinch yourself," he said.

POLY-TICKS

With the presidential campaigns really starting to heat up, it is somewhat ironic that, even with all the energy and excitement being generated, people continue to hold politics and politicians in such low regard. Well, hell, they deserve it. Politics today consists of more lawbreakers than lawmakers and it's the only field in which the more experience you have, the worse you get. The two-party system, which I call the Crips and the Bloods, has pretty much become the same guy admiring himself in the mirror.

Our government, unfortunately, has also become a government of the money, by the money, and for the money. If you don't believe me, just try forgetting your checkbook and seeing if you can get into your congressman's office. Another reason people distrust politicians and politics today goes all the way back to George Washington's time. George believed that all government and politics needed was "common sense and common honesty." Sadly, these two precious commodities are precisely what's lacking today in our elected officials.

These are only a few of the reasons that have goosed me into coming up with my own definition of politics. It goes as follows: *Poly* means more than one, and *ticks* are blood-sucking parasites. Throughout my campaign for governor of Texas I often contended that musicians could run the government better than politicians. We wouldn't get a lot done in the morning, I said, but we'd work late and we'd be honest. Frankly, *beauticians* could run the government better than politicians. So could opticians, magicians, or morticians—anybody from outside of politics is going to be a damn sight better at getting the train back on track than the ones on the inside who put her in the ditch to begin with.

First as a musician, then as an author, I've traveled all over this great state, and I know that I'm more in touch and in tune with real Texans than are most politicians. Think of the last time you were truly inspired by a politician. Think of the last time you really respected one. And think of the last time a politician really respected you.

I've hung out often in my life in rooms full of musicians and now I can also claim—though it's quite far from a brag—that I've also hung out in rooms full of politicians. There's a basic, almost palpable difference between the two groups. The musicians have honesty, integrity, humanity, creativity, and a sense of humor. The politicians, as a general rule, have none of these qualities in any great degree. They lack creative solutions to problems, they are shallow and superficial by their very nature, and they all appear to have humor bypasses. Whether they are big stars or virtually unknown, the musicians all seem to evoke a basic sense of decency, a trait noticeably lacking in most politicians.

One of the first people I often seek advice from and, indeed, tapped to be an integral part of the campaign, was Willie Nelson, whom I like to call "The Hillbilly Dalai Lama." For as long as I've known him, he's been rather far to the left of me, not to mention quite a bit higher than me. This was especially true just before the invasion of Iraq when Willie and I were discussing the matter on his bus. To his credit, Willie was against the war from the very beginning. He thought it was a bad idea altogether. I, on the other hand, felt it might be a good idea to knock a dictator off and make the other dictators look over their shoulders a bit.

As we were discussing whether it was a sound plan to invade Iraq, I recall the conversation becoming increasingly animated. Willie, I remember, was smoking a joint about the size of a large kosher salami, and I was getting more and more frustrated trying to get through to him. Finally, I said, "Look, Willie. The guy is a tyrannical bully and we've got to take him out!"

"No," said Willie. "He's our president and we've got to stand by him."

In late 2004, as I was deciding whether or not to officially throw my hat in the ring, I went to see Willie again to get his blessings and any advice or suggestions he might bestow upon me. He was on the bus writing a new song called "I Hate Every Bone In Your Body Except Mine" and smoking a joint the size of a large cedar fence post.

"Willie," I said, "I've got a great life and, as much as I love Texas, I'm not sure if I want to sacrifice it on the altar of politics. On the other hand, we haven't had an independent candidate even get on the ballot in 154 years and this may be the last opportunity of our lifetimes to make this happen."

"And your name is?" Willie said.

After a while we settled down into a discussion of the fact that, for the first time in history, the great state of Texas was importing energy. Willie laid out a highly persuasive argument for biodiesel and agreed to be my energy czar if the people of Texas had the vision to elect me governor. The fact that Willie has a special rapport with farmers was not lost upon the Kinkster. With Willie in charge, farmers' biodiesel co-ops would be springing up all over Texas to make biodiesel readily available to everyone. And, as I went on to often point out in stump speeches all over the state, Willie would be different from the current crop of bureaucrats. He would never have his hand in Texas's pocket.

The more we talked and dreamed, the more we realized that these were two reachable stars—clean energy and clean government. Energy would be Willie's star—fuel you could actually grow. Clean government would be mine—throw the money-changers out of the temple. From inside Willie's tour bus we saw what we believed could be a new and beautiful Texas—a

Texas that would not be forever following behind but soon would be leading the American parade. It was a wonderful dream, and, like all dreams, we figured, there was a chance it might come true.

Before I left, Willie had even come up with a new campaign slogan for me. It was catchy and clever and would soon be ringing out from Amarillo to Brownsville. It was, "Criticize me all you want, but don't circumcise me anymore."

TWO JACKS

A villain, a patriot, and a scoundrel. Here's to my spiritual role model, Jack Ruby, the original Texas Jewboy.

On November 22, 1963—the fateful day that shook the world, the day that caused Walter Cronkite to shed a tear on national television, the day that belied Nellie Connally's encouraging words, "You can't say Dallas doesn't love you, Mr. President," the day that gave Oliver Stone an idea for a screenplay—I was a freshman at the University of Texas, sleeping off a beer party from the night before. Indeed, I slept through the assassination of John F. Kennedy like a bad dream and, upon waking, retained one seemingly nonsensical phrase: "Texas Cookbook Suppository."

It was only later, once I'd sobered up, that I realized I'd been sleeping not only through history class but history itself. I'd also slept through anthropology class, where I'd received some rather caustic remarks from my red-bearded professor for a humorous monograph I'd written on the Flathead Indians of Montana. I'd gotten an A on the paper, along with the comment, "Your style has got to go." But I realized that he was wrong. Style is everything in this world. JFK's style made him who he was. Even dead, he had a lingering charisma that caused me to join the Peace Corps. Yet it was the style of another man in Dallas that was to change my life, I now believe, even more profoundly. I'm referring, of course, to that patriot, that hero, that villain, that famously flamboyant scoundrel, Jack Ruby.

Like the first real cowboy spotted by a child, Ruby made an indelible impression upon my youthful consciousness. He was the first Texas Jewboy I ever saw. There he stood, like a good cowboy, like a good Jew, wearing his hat indoors, shooting the bad guy who'd killed the president and doing it right there on live TV. Never mind that the bad guy had yet to be indicted or convicted; never mind that he was a captive in handcuffs carefully "guarded" by the Dallas cops. Those are mere details relegated to the footnotes and footprints of history. Ruby had done what every good God-fearing, red-blooded American had wished he could do. And he was one of our boys!

Ten years later, in 1973, with Ruby still in mind as a spiritual role model, I formed the band Kinky Friedman and the Texas Jewboys, which would traverse the width and breadth of the land, celebrated, castigated, and one night nearly castrated after a show in Nacogdoches. None of it would have happened, I feel sure, without the influence of Jack Ruby, that bastard child of twin cultures, death-bound and desperately determined to leave his mark on the world. While many saw Ruby as a caricature or a buffoon, I saw in him the perfect blending of East and West— the Jew, forever seeking the freedom to be who he was, and the cowboy, forever craving that same metaphysical elbow room. I, perhaps naively, perceived him as a member of two lost tribes, each a vanishing breed, each blessed, cursed, and chosen to wander.

In the days and months that followed the assassination, as Ruby languished in jail, the world learned more about this vigilante visionary, this angst-ridden avenging angel. Ruby, it emerged, was indubitably an interesting customer. He owned a strip club in which the girls adored him and in which he would periodically punch out unruly patrons. This cowboy exuberance was invariably followed by Jewish guilt. Josh Alan Friedman, a guitar virtuoso who is as close to a biographer as Ruby probably has, notes that Jack was known to pay medical and dental bills for his punch-out victims and offer them free patronage at his strip club. With Lee Harvey Oswald, however, this beneficence was not in evidence. According to Friedman, Ruby was utterly without remorse over Oswald's death, delighting in the bags of fan mail he received in his prison cell.

In time the mail petered out and, not long after that, so did Ruby. He died a bitter man, possibly the last living piece in a puzzle only God or Agatha Christie could have created. I didn't really blame Ruby for being somewhat bitter. The way I saw it, he *had* actually accomplished something in killing Oswald. He'd helped one neurotic Jew, namely myself, come up with a pretty good name for his band.

Years after Ruby had gone to that grassy knoll in the sky, my friend Mickey Raphael, who plays blues harp with Willie Nelson, tried to get a gig at Jack's old strip club. At the time, Mickey had a jug band, and though he found the place to be redolent of Ruby's spirit, he didn't get the gig. "I thought you guys *liked* jugs," Mickey told the manager.

Thus is the legacy of one little man determined to take the law into his own little hand. And so they will go together into history, a pair of Jacks, one dealt a fatal blow in the prime of his life, the other dealt from the bottom of the deck; one remembered with the passion of an eternal flame, the other all but forgotten. Friedman notes that Ruby wept for Kennedy. Chet Flippo, in his definitive book *Your Cheatin' Heart,* tells of Ruby's friendship and loyalty a decade earlier toward another one of life's great death-bound passengers, Hank Williams. Ruby, according to Flippo, was one of the last promoters to continue to book Hank as the legend drunkenly, tragically struggled to get out of this world alive. He was also one of the few human beings on the planet who knew Hank Williams *and* spoke Yiddish.

Was Ruby a slightly weather-beaten patriotic hero? Was he a sleazeball with a heart of gold? Was he, to paraphrase Leonard Cohen, just another Joseph, following a star, trying to find a manger in Dallas? My old pal Vaughn Meader, who in the early sixties recorded the hugely successful *The First Family* album

CALLAHAN

satirizing JFK, probably expressed it best. After flying for most of that tragic day, oblivious to the news, he got into a taxi at the airport in Milwaukee. The driver asked him, "Did you hear about the president getting shot?" "No," said Vaughn. "How does it go?"

HERO ANAGRAMS

———◆———

Bob Dylan: Bland boy—nobly bad

Hank Williams: Sank all whim

Willie Nelson: I swell online—nine oil wells

Oscar Wilde: Cowards lie—lad cries ow

Father Damien: Renamed faith

Jack Ruby: Back jury

Arthur Conan Doyle: Can try unload hero

Sherlock Holmes: Hell mocks heroes

Billy Joe Shaver: Behave, sir jolly—shy jovial rebel

ODE TO BILLY JOE

If Carl Sandburg had come from Waco, his name would have been Billy Joe Shaver. Back in the late sixties, when Christ was a cowboy, I first met Billy Joe in Nashville. We were both songwriters, and we once stayed up for six nights and it felt like a week. Today, he's arguably the finest poet and songwriter this state has ever produced.

If you doubt my opinion, you could ask Willie Nelson or wait until you get to hillbilly heaven to ask Townes Van Zandt, who are the other folks in the equation, but they might not give you a straight answer. Willie, for instance, tends to speak only in lyrics. Just last week I was with an attractive young woman, and I said to Willie, "I'm not sure who's taller, but her ass is six inches higher than mine." He responded, "My ass is higher than both of your asses." Be that as it may, you'll rarely see Willie perform without singing Billy Joe's classic "I Been to Georgia on a Fast Train," which contains the line "I'd just like to mention that my grandma's old-age pension is the reason why I'm standin' here today." Like everything else about Billy Joe, that line is the literal truth. He is an achingly honest story-teller in a world that prefers to hear something else.

Thanks to his grandma's pension, Billy Joe survived grinding poverty as a child in Corsicana. "*Course* I cana!" was his motto then, but after his grandma conked, he moved to Waco, where he built a résumé that would've made Jack London mildly petulant. He worked as a cowboy, a roughneck, a cotton picker, a chicken plucker, and a millworker (he lost three fingers at that job when he was twenty-two. Later he wrote these lines:

Three fingers' whiskey pleasures the drinker
Movin' does more than the drinkin' for me
Willy he tells me that doers and thinkers
Say movin's the closest thing to being free.

I believe that every culture gets what it deserves. Ours deserves Rush Limbaugh and Dr. Laura and Garth Brooks (whom I like to refer to as the anti-Hank). But when the meaningless mainstream is forgotten, people will still remember those who struggled with success: van Gogh and Mozart, who were buried in paupers' graves; Hank, who died in the back of a Cadillac; and Anne Frank, who had no grave at all. I think there may be room in that shining motel of immortality for Billy Joe's timeless

CALLAHAN

"Miss Gordon, please live my life for me."

works, beautiful beyond words and music, written by a gypsy guitarist with three fingers missing.

Last February Billy Joe and I teamed up again to play a series of shows with Little Jewford, Jesse "Guitar" Taylor, "Sweet" Mary Hattersley, and my Lebanese friend Jimmie "Ratso" Silman. (Ratso and I have long considered ourselves to be the last true hope for peace in the Middle East.) Pieces were missing, however. God had sent a hat trick of grief to Billy Joe in a year that even Job would have thrown back. His mother, Victory, and his beloved wife, Brenda, stepped on a rainbow, and on New Year's Eve, 2000, his son, Eddy, a sweet and talented guitarist, joined them. Hank and Townes also had been bugled to Jesus in the cosmic window of the New Year.

I watched Billy Joe playing with pain, the big man engendering, perhaps not so strangely, an almost Judy Garland–like rapport with the audience. He played "Ol' Five and Dimers

Like Me" (which Dylan recorded), "You Asked Me To" (which Elvis recorded), and "Honky Tonk Heroes" (which Waylon recorded). He also played one of my favorites, which, well, Billy Joe recorded:

> Our freckled faces sparkled then like diamonds in the
>   rough
> With smiles that smelled of snaggled teeth and good ol'
>   Garrett snuff
> If I could I would be tradin' all this fat back for the lean
> When Jesus was our savior and cotton was our king.

Seeing Billy Joe perform that night reminded me of a benefit we'd played in Kerrville several years before. Friends had asked me to help them save the old Arcadia Theatre, and I called upon Billy Joe. Toward the end of his set, however, a rather uncomfortable moment occurred when he told the crowd, "There's one man I'd like to thank at this time." I, of course, began making my way to the stage. "That man is the reason I'm here tonight," he said.

I confidently walked in front of the whole crowd, preparing to leap onstage when he mentioned my name. "That man," said Billy Joe, "is Jesus Christ."

Much chagrined, I walked back to my seat as the audience aimed their laughter at me like the Taliban militia shooting down a Buddha. It was quite a social embarrassment for the Kinkster. But I'll get over it.

So will Billy Joe.

THE BACK OF
THE BUS

I met Willie Nelson on the gangplank of Noah's Ark. Like
most country music friendships, ours has managed to
remain close because we've stayed the hell away from each
other. I've played a few of Willie's picnics and we've attended
the same Tupperware parties now and then, but ironically,
I didn't really start feeling spiritually akin to him until I'd
phased out of country music almost entirely and become a
pointy-headed intellectual mystery writer. Now that my novel
Roadkill features Willie as a main character, our karma is
suddenly linked—whether we like it or not.

Even when Willie produced a record of mine in Nashville in
1974 (and sang backup with Waylon Jennings and Tompall
Glaser on "They Ain't Makin' Jews Like Jesus Anymore"), he

and I were still only close enough for country dancin'. Of course, we'd come from different backgrounds. Willie had picked cotton in the fields as a kid in Abbott. For entertainment and income from local farmers, he'd go out with a little homemade paddle and kill bumblebees; he would come home looking like he'd just fought fifteen rounds with God. Willie grew up never having much money or much schooling and got married and divorced about ninety-seven times. All he ever wanted to do was write songs and sing them for people and maybe get one of those cars that roared down the highway with the windows rolled up in the middle of summer, indicating that the driver could afford that ultimate symbol of success; air-conditioning.

By the time Willie finally got that car, it was about ten minutes too late to make any difference, but he did get something else far more important: He got a bus. In fact, he got three buses. The one he lives in and calls home is known as the Honeysuckle Rose. The way I first really got to know Willie was by traveling with him aboard the Honeysuckle Rose. It's a floating city unto itself, with "floating" the operative word. Even the secondhand smoke has been known to make casual visitors mildly amphibious. (There is no truth, incidentally, to the widely held belief that Willie needs the other two buses to carry all the weed he smokes on the first bus.) By contrast, my own country music career never quite reached the tour-bus level. The closest I came was a blue Beauville van, out of which the Texas Jewboys poured like a thousand clowns at every honky-tonk, minstrel show, whorehouse, bar, and bar mitzvah throughout the South, to paraphrase Jerry Jeff Walker. The Beauville, like my career, was not a vehicle destined for vastly commercial country music stardom, though it did have at least one good quality: It broke down in all the right places.

Also unlike Willie, I came from an upper-middle-class home, which is always a hard cross for a country singer to bear. I got a guitar as a young teenager in Houston, and like Townes Van Zandt, the first song I learned was "Fraulein." By then Willie and his sister, Bobbie, were already playing in beer halls on Saturday nights and in church the next morning. By the time I had my bar mitzvah, Willie had sold Bibles and written "Family Bible," which he also sold, reportedly for fifty dollars.

Willie never went to college, but I graduated from the University of Texas's highly advanced Plan II liberal arts program. Then I joined the Peace Corps and worked in the jungles of Borneo, while Willie continued writing, singing, marrying, divorcing, struggling, and smoking. Like I said, I don't really know what Willie and I have in common—other than the fact that we're both pretty fair bumblebee fighters. Probably it has to do with what Johnny Gimble, the great country fiddle player, told me once aboard the Honeysuckle Rose. He said that when he was a kid he'd told his mother, "Mama, when I grow up, I'm gonna be a musician." His mother had answered, "Make up your mind, son, because you can't do both."

If Willie had been Rosa Parks, there never would have been a civil rights movement in this country because he refuses to leave his soulful locus at the back of the bus unless it's to go on-stage or onto a golf course. Golf is a passion with Willie, and it's the one aspect of his life I find stultifyingly dull. As I once told Willie, "The only two good balls I ever hit was when I stepped on the garden rake." Willie, of course, responded to this news with a golf anecdote. He told me about a woman who'd recently come off his golf course at Briarcliff, went into the pro shop, and complained to the golf pro that she'd been stung by a bee. "Where'd it sting you?" asked the pro. "Between the first and second holes," she said. "Well I can tell you right now," said the golf pro, "your stance is too wide."

After writing a number of mystery novels and traveling extensively with Willie, the idea crossed my dusty desk to write a book with him as a central character, set the scene aboard the Honeysuckle Rose, and let the bus take the story wherever the hell it went. This meant I would be exchanging my New York loft with the cat and the lesbian dance class above for Willie and his crew. Willie had never been a character in a murder mystery, but he thought it might be worth a shot, so to speak.

We crisscrossed the country together. As the song goes: "Cowboys Are Frequently Secretly Fond of Each Other." Willie sang, played chess, and smoked enough dope to make him so high that he had to call NASA to find his head. As for myself, I smoked cigars, drank a little Chateau de Catpiss, played chess with Willie, and wrote down many things at all hours of the day and night in my little private investigator's notebook. Along the way, I went to many of Willie's shows. Wandering around backstage at a Willie Nelson concert is a bit like being the parrot on the shoulder of the guy who's running the Ferris wheel. It's not the best seat in the house, but you see enough lights, action, people, and confusion to make you wonder if anybody knows what the hell's going on. If you're sitting out in front, of course, it all rolls along as smoothly as a German train schedule, but as Willie, like any great magician, would be the first to point out, the real show is never in the center ring.

Backstage at any show has its similarities, whether it's Broadway or the circus or the meanest little honky-tonk in Nacogdoches—the palpable sense of people out there somewhere in the darkness waiting for your performance, or being able to pull a curtain back slightly and experience the actual sight of the audience sitting there waiting to be entertained by someone who, in this case, happens to be you. It's the reason Richard Burton vomited before almost every live performance of his life. It's part of the reason George Jones took Early Times, Judy Garland took bluebirds, and many a shining star burned out too soon. Standing alone in the spotlight, up on the high wire without a net, is something Willie Nelson has had to deal with for most of his adult life.

One night at Billy Bob's in Fort Worth, I was standing backstage in the near darkness when a voice right behind me almost caused me to drop my cigar into my Dr Pepper. It was Willie. "Let me show you something," he said, and he pulled a curtain back, revealing a cranked-up crowd beginning to get drunk, beginning to grow restless, and packed in tighter than smoked oysters in Hong Kong. Viewed from our hidden angle, they were a strangely intimidating sight, yet Willie took them in almost like a walk in the trailer park.

"That's where the real show is," he said.

"If that's where the real show is," I said, "I want my money back."

"Do you realize," Willie continued in a soft, soothing, serious voice, "that ninety-nine percent of those people are not with their true first choice?"

He looked out at the crowd for a moment or two longer. Then he let the curtain drop from his hand, sending us back into twilight.

"That's why they play the jukebox," he said.

Willie's character leapt off the stage and onto the page. I don't know if you'd call it Jewish radar or cowboy intuition, but during my travels with Willie, a story line began to evolve. He would be at the center of one of my most challenging cases. There wasn't a butler to do it, but Willie did have a valet named Ben Dorsey, who'd once been John Wayne's valet. This provided some humorous commentary, since Willie wasn't an enormous fan of the Duke's. Willie preferred the old singing cowboys. Of John Wayne he once said, "He couldn't sing and his horse was never smart." (That kind of talk never failed to irritate Dorsey and usually resulted in some sort of tension convention.) Other real characters who inhabit the Honeysuckle Rose and the pages of *Roadkill* are Bobbie Nelson, Willie's sister; Lana Nelson, Willie's daughter; Gates "Gator" Moore, his intrepid bus driver; L. G., his one-man security team; and a cast of thousands of friends, fans, and family, who, along with life itself, did everything they could to interrupt our chess games.

You can tell a lot about a man by his chess game, unless, of course, your opponent is smoking a joint the size of Long Island.

Edgar Allan Poe once said of chess: "It is complex without being profound," and it is because of that very complexity that a momentary loss of concentration or the entry of some foreign emotion, like a broken heart, can torpedo the game. When you take this into consideration, Willie plays with the evenness of the Mahatma, at a lightninglike pace, and rarely loses. (I, of course, rarely lose either.)

One of the things I admire most about the way Willie plays the game of chess, as well as the game of life, is his Zen Texan approach to inevitable triumphs and defeats. The endgame doesn't hold great interest for him because he's already thinking about the next game. If he comes off less than his best in one game, one show, one interview, one album, his next effort is invariably brilliant. This is one of the reasons I've always looked up to both Willie Nelson and Bob Dylan, even though

BEST-LOVED POSSUM TUNES.

...ON THE ROAD AGAIN...

CALLAHAN

they're both shorter than everyone except Paul Simon, who I also look up to.

I see Willie as a storybook gingerbread man: born into poverty, rich in the coin of the spirit, ephemeral and timeless, fragile and strong, beautiful beyond words and music, healing the broken hearts of other people and sometimes, just maybe, his own as well. Yesterday's wine for Willie includes personal tragedies, Internal Revenue Service audits, and a somewhat geriatric band that has been around forever yet to this very day undeniably takes no prisoners. The changing landscape of country music has made major-label support and generous radio airplay almost a thing of the past. For many legends of country music, this trendy tidal wave toward Nashville poster boys and modern, youthful "hat acts," plus the inevitable pull of the old rocking chair, has meant the end of careers that were supposed to last forever.

In the midst of all this, like a diamond amongst the rhinestones, Willie Nelson stays on the road.

LOTTIE'S LOVE

When Lottie Cotton was born, on September 6, 1902, in the tiny Southeast Texas town of Liberty, there were no airplanes in the sky. There were no SUVs, no super-highways, no cell phones, no televisions. When Lottie was laid to rest in Houston, there was a black Jesus looking after her from the wall of the funeral chapel. Many biblical scholars agree to-day that Jesus, being of North African descent, very likely may have been black. But Lottie was always spiritually color-blind; her Jesus was the color of love. She spent her entire life looking after others. One of them, I'm privileged to say, was me.

Lottie was not a maid. She was not a nanny. She did not live with us. We were not rich rug rats raised in River Oaks. We lived in a middle-class neighborhood of Houston. My mother and father both worked. Lottie helped cook and baby-sit during the day and soon became part of our family.

I was old enough to realize yet young enough to know that I was in the presence of a special person. Laura Bush, my occasional pen pal, had this to say about Lottie in a recent letter, and I don't think she'd mind my sharing it with you: "Only special ladies earn the title of 'second mother.' She must have been a remarkable person, and I know you miss her."

There are not many people like Lottie left in this world. Few of us, indeed, have the time and the love to spend our days and nights looking after others. Most of us take our responsibilities to our own families seriously. Many of us work hard at our jobs. Some of us even do unto others as we would have them do unto us. But how many would freely, willingly, lovingly roam the cottonfields of the heart with two young boys and a young girl, a cocker spaniel named Rex, and a white mouse named Archimedes?

One way or another for almost fifty-five years, wherever I traveled in the world, Lottie and I managed to stay in touch. I now calculate that when Lottie sent me birthday cards in Borneo when I was in the Peace Corps, she was in her early sixties, an age that I myself am now rapidly, if disbelievingly, approaching. She also remained in touch with my brother, Roger, who lives in Maryland, and my sister, Marcie, who lives in Vietnam. To live a hundred years on this troubled planet is a rare feat, but to maintain contact with your "children" for all that length of time, and for them to have become your dear friends in later years, is rarer still.

For Lottie did not survive one century in merely the clinical sense; she was as sharp as a tack until the end of her days. At the ripe young age of ninety-nine, she could sit at the kitchen table and discuss politics or religion—or stuffed animals. Lottie left behind an entire menagerie of teddy bears and other stuffed animals, each of them with a name and personality all its own. She also left behind two live animals, dogs named Minnie and Little Dog, who had followed her and protected her everywhere she went. Minnie is a little dog named for my mother, and Little Dog, as might be expected, is a big dog.

Lottie is survived by her daughter, Ada Beverly (the two of them have referred to each other as "Mama" for at least the past thirty years), and one grandson, Jeffery. She's also survived by Roger, Marcie, and me, who live scattered about a modern-day world, a world that has gained so much in technology yet seems to have lost those sacred recipes for popcorn balls and chocolate-chip cookies. "She was a seasoned saint," a young preacher who had never met her said at her funeral. But was it too late, I wondered, to bless the hands that prepared the food? And there were so many other talents in Lottie's gentle hands, not the least of which was the skill to be a true mender of the human spirit.

I don't know what else you can say about someone who has been in your life forever, someone who was always there for you, even when "there" was far away. Lottie was my mother's friend, she was my friend, and now she has a friend in Jesus. She always had a friend in Jesus, come to think of it. The foundation of her faith was as strong as the foundation for the railroad tracks she helped lay as a young girl in Liberty. Lottie, you've outlived your very bones, darling. Yours is not the narrow immortality craved by the authors, actors, and artists of this world. Yours is the immortality of a precious passenger on the train to glory, which has taken you from the cross ties on the railroad to the stars in the sky.

By day and by night, each in their turn, the sun and the moon gaze through the window, now and again reflecting upon the gold and silver pathways of childhood. The pathways are still there, but we cannot see them with our eyes, nor shall we ever again tread lightly upon them with our feet. Yet as children, we never suspect we might someday lose our way. We think we have all the time in the world.

I am still here, Lottie. And Ada gave me two of the teddy bears that I sent you long ago. As I write these words, those bears sit on the windowsill looking after me. Some might say they are only stuffed animals. But, Lottie, you and I know what's really inside them. It's the stuff of dreams.

PART III

ADVICE ON WRITING

KILLING ME SOFTLY

Why would the author of a successful series of mystery novels featuring himself as the central character want to commit literary suicide by killing off his hero? Is the author, who happens to be named Kinky Friedman, subconsciously jealous of the fictional fame garnered around the world by the character, who also happens to be named Kinky Friedman? Have author and character melded into a psychotic, schizophrenic entity so clinically ill as to obscure the difference between important clues like cocaine and horseradish? Both of us are glad you asked. The truth is, by the time you've written your seventeenth mystery novel, if you ain't crazy, there's something wrong with you. If you happen to be your own main character, it tends to be even worse.

There are some things that the two of you may have in common, of course. You both may smoke Cuban cigars. You both may drink Jameson Irish whiskey. But, after a time, the bad outweighs the good. It doesn't take long to discover, for instance, that the real you and the fabricated you both seem to lust after the same kind of woman. Once a woman's imagination has been captured by a fictional heartthrob, the flesh-and-blood version has a hard act to follow. I'm not the first novelist who's felt the need to kill a character better known and better regarded than he is.

In 1893 *The Final Problem* recorded the passing of the legendary detective Sherlock Holmes. The man who offed Holmes was the same man who created him, Sir Arthur Conan Doyle. Why did it have to end this way, with Holmes and his archenemy, Moriarty, representing the forces of good and evil in the world, struggling in each other's grasp, then plunging to their deaths at Reichenbach Falls? Was Conan Doyle weary of his celebrated sleuth, or was the author in such a petulant snit about being eclipsed by his invention that he murdered him in a fit of literary pique? Or did Conan Doyle destroy Holmes because, as Oscar Wilde famously wrote, "each man kills the thing he loves"? The difference between the artist and the murderer, Holmes himself once said, is that the artist knows when to stop. My latest mystery, *Ten Little New Yorkers,* will also be my last. It's not that I'm fresh out of mad nights or candle wax or typewriter ribbons; it's merely that I'm running low on the desperation that makes a writer good in the first place. The mystery field, one quickly discovers, is as narrow as it is deep: The elements that are essential to a mystery are the same ones that often keep it trite and limited. As an author, you're constantly trying to fool the reader without cheating him. Your best writing is rarely about smoke and mirrors or the corpse in the library. More often it deals with the dreams of a detective who wonders if there's life before death. The mystery of life, in other words, is a greater and more compelling story than the cheap, dog-eared mystery of death. Life is hanging on tight, spurring hard, and letting 'er buck. Death is merely letting go of the saddle horn.

When I wrote my first mystery, *Greenwich Killing Time,* in 1984, I never dreamed the series would continue for more than twenty years. Long before that, I suspected, the reader would tire of my cleverness. I hoped, naturally, that there would be more than one reader, and in time my hopes were realized.

Today my mysteries have been translated into more languages than there are books in the series, including, recently, Russian, Hebrew, and Japanese. I can't imagine what these people think when they read them. Then again, I can't imagine what I was thinking when I wrote them.

In *Ten Little New Yorkers,* Manhattan is victimized by a string of vicious murders. Not much of a plot, you might say, but when you've written as many of these boogers as I have, you begin to understand why plots are for cemeteries. And speaking of cemeteries, it was clearly time to plant Kinky Friedman and his colorful band of flatulent friends. If I didn't kill him soon, I knew I ran the risk of becoming a literary hack—a bitter, jaundiced, humorless, insular, constipated prig, like most successful authors. I preferred to stay the way I'd always been: obliviously well adjusted to a profoundly sick society.

Having decided to do away with Kinky Friedman, one nagging question remained: Which Kinky should I kill? The character, with his bizarre behavior, tediously eccentric mannerisms, and cloying colloquial language, was now locked in such a hopelessly convoluted love-hate relationship with the author that it might require dental records, or maybe a rectal probe, to tell them apart. The last guy with an invention named for him was Dr. Frankenstein, and everybody knows what happened there. I had created a monster, so now I had to destroy it. So Kinky the cat-loving, cigar-smoking amateur sleuth meets his maker at the end of *Ten Little New Yorkers.* I had no choice; it was spiritual self-defense. Much like the great Holmes, the fictional Kinkster dies in a fall from a bridge while grappling with the murderer. While his death is liberating to me personally, it does not gladden my heart. In an odd sort of way, I was almost starting to like the guy.

If you happen to be a frustrated fan of the fictional Friedman, I can only say that even Conan Doyle was eventually forced by pressure from his readers to bring Holmes back to life. If, indeed, I hear the literary community clamoring for Kinky's return, I may have to follow suit. Sometimes, in my dreams, I think I hear them beginning to clamor. When I wake up to the nonfiction world, however, I realize it was only the sound of one hand clapping.

FICTIONAL CHARACTERS KILLED OFF BY THEIR CREATORS

Sherlock Holmes: one of the best known and most universally recognizable literary characters in any genre. Sherlock Holmes was a fictional detective of the late nineteenth and early twentieth centuries, who first appeared in publication in 1887. He was created by Scottish author and physician Sir Arthur Conan Doyle. Holmes lived in London and was famous for his genius at solving the most difficult cases with his brilliant use of deductive reasoning and keen observation skills. He had a profound knowledge of chemistry, was a competent cryptanalyst, and was skilled in boxing, swordsmanship, clever disguises, and the violin. Holmes disliked contemplating anything that would clutter up his memory and get in the way of his detective work. He had a flair for showmanship and enjoyed staging dramatic endings to his cases for the benefit of Watson or Scotland Yard. Holmes described himself and his habits as "Bohemian." Holmes' friend and biographer, Dr. John H. Watson, said that Holmes's only vice was an occasional use of cocaine and morphine.

Sir Arthur Conan Doyle killed off Holmes in "*The Final Problem*," which appeared in print in 1893. After resisting public pressure to resurrect Holmes, Conan Doyle brought him back to life ten years later and continued to write Holmes stories for a quarter-century longer.

Chewbacca: Del Rey publishing company won the license to the "Star Wars" books from Bantam a few years ago and decided to launch a new series called "New Jedi Order," based on George Lucas's Star Wars universe. Fantasy writer R. A. Salvatore was chosen to write the first novel in the series, *Vector Prime*. In this book, he killed off Chewbacca, the beloved Wookiee partner of Han Solo. Lucas gave his approval to Chewbacca's death, but it ignited a storm of controversy from Star Wars fans. Despite this, the book went on to be a best-seller, and Salvatore was subsequently picked to write the novelization of *Star Wars: Episode II—Attack of the Clones*.

Hercule Poirot: For more than half a century, Dame Agatha Christie was the foremost British writer of mystery novels. Her books have been translated into every major language and her two creations, Detective Poirot and Miss Jane Marple, are world famous. Hercule Poirot, the Belgian detective created by Dame Agatha Christie, first appeared in the novel *The Mysterious Affair at Styles* in 1920. He was the main character in more than thirty novels and fifty short stories. Despite Poirot's popularity with her fans, by 1930 Agatha Christie found Poirot "insufferable" and by 1960, she felt that he was a "detestable, bombastic, tiresome, egocentric little creep."

Still the public loved him, and Christie refused to kill him off, claiming that it was her duty to produce what the public liked, and what the public liked was Poirot. In 1975 a year before her own death, Christie killed off Poirot in the novel *Curtain: Poirot's Last Case*. Poirot died from inevitable complications of a heart condition; by this point in his life he was wearing a wig and a false moustache, and also seemed to be afflicted by arthritis.

Captain America: The alter ego of Steve Rogers, he was a superhero in the Marvel Comics universe. Created by Joe Simon and Jack Kirby, Captain America was one of the most popular characters of Marvel Comics's predecessor, Timely Comics; he made his first appearance in December 1940, a year before the bombing of Pearl Harbor. With his sidekick, Bucky, Captain America faced Nazis, Japanese, and other threats to wartime America. He remained popular throughout the forties but by the early fifties, sales dropped off and Captain America eventually disappeared after 1954. He returned in 1964 when it was explained that in the final days of WWII, Captain America fell from an experimental drone plane into the North Atlantic Ocean and spent decades frozen in a state of suspended animation. During the 1970s, the hero found a new generation of readers as leader of the all-star superhero team the Avengers.

In April 2007, Captain America's alter ego Steve Rogers was shot by a sniper outside of a federal courthouse and later died at the hospital. The character's death was reported on major news outlets like CNN and the Associated Press. His death came as a blow to ninety-three-year-old cocreator Joe Simon, who said, "It's a hell of a time for him to go. We really need him now."

TALENT

L ike the tides, the seasons, and the Bandera branch of the Jehovah's Witnesses, the Texas Book Festival is coming around again, allowing us to meet authors we love, hate, or very possibly, find a little ho-hum. I always look forward to the book festival because it provides me with the spiritual soapbox to give advice to other authors, an audience that, predictably, has never learned to listen. Conversely, I've never learned to pull my lips together, so the system works. My advice to authors, and the misguided multitudes who want to be authors, is a variation on a truthful if sometimes tedious theme. "Talent," I tell them in stentorian tones, "is its own reward. If you're unlucky enough to have it, don't expect anything else." These wise words, of course, come from a man who's spent his entire professional career trying to eclipse Leon Redbone.

My theory is that in all areas of creative human endeavor, the presence of true talent is almost always the kiss of death. It's no accident that three of the people who were tragically forced into bankruptcy at the end of their lives were Edgar Allan Poe, Oscar Wilde, and Mark Twain. It's no fluke of fate that Schubert died shortly after giving the world the *Unfinished Symphony*. You probably wouldn't have finished it either if you had syphilis and twelve cents in your pocket. Or how would you like to have died at age twenty-nine in the backseat of a Cadillac? If you're Hank Williams, that's what talent got you. But what *is* talent? And why would anyone in his right mind want it? As Albert Einstein often said, "I don't know."

In fact, talent is such a difficult quality to identify or define that we frequently end up losing it in the lights, relegating it at last to the trash bin, the cheap motel, the highway, the gutter, or the cross. Indeed, if you look with an objective eye at the *New York Times* Best-Seller List, the *Billboard* music charts, and the highest-rated network TV offerings, the one thing they seem to have in common is an absence of original creative expression, i.e., talent.

My editor says I'm one of the most talented writers he knows. The problem is that even if I have talent, I don't know what it is—and if I did, I'd get rid of it immediately. Then I'd be on my way to vast commercial success. Talent, however, is a bit like God; you never see it, but there are moments when you're pretty sure it's there. So because I can't clinically isolate it, I'm stuck with all my wonderful talent, and the most practical thing I can do is start looking for a sturdy bridge to sleep under or a gutter in a good neighborhood.

If you have a little talent, you're probably all right. Let's say you're good at building bird houses or you play the bagpipes or, like my fairy godmother, Edythe Kruger, you do an almost uncanny impersonation of the duck on the AFLAC commercial. These kinds of narrow little talents have never harmed a soul, nor kept anyone from living a successful, happy life. It's when you're afflicted with that raw, shimmering, innate talent—talent with a big "T"—that you can really get into trouble. Remember that Judy Garland died broke on the toilet. Lenny Bruce also died broke on the toilet. Jim Morrison, just to be perverse, died fairly well financially fixed at the age of twenty-seven in a Paris bathtub. Elvis also died on the toilet, but definitely he wasn't broke. Along with a vast fortune, he had well over a million dollars in a checking account that drew no interest. Who cares about money, he figured, when you've got talent? I myself was a chess prodigy, playing a match with world grandmaster Samuel Reschevsky when I was only seven years old. It's been downhill from there. These days I find myself constipated most of the time and I never take a bath.

They say it takes more talent to spot talent than it does to have talent. Conversely, it's easy to know when it isn't there, although someone without talent rarely notices its absence. Some friends of mine had a band once, and they went to audition for a talent scout in his office. The talent scout said, "Okay, let's see what you can do." The leader of the band began to pick his nose while playing the French horn. Another guy started beating out the rhythm on his own buttocks while projectile vomiting on the man's desk. The other two members of the band jumped simultaneously onto the desk and began unabashedly engaging in an act too graphic to describe here. "I've seen enough," shouted the talent scout in disgust. "What do you call this act anyway?" The French horn player stopped playing the instrument and stopped picking his nose. "We call ourselves," he said, "The Aristocrats."

Another example of what might help define talent takes us back to Polyclitus, the famous sculptor in ancient Greece. Polyclitus, it is said, once sculped two statues at the same time: one in his living room, in public view, and one in his bedroom, which he worked on privately and kept wrapped in a tarpaulin. When visitors came by, they would comment on the public work, saying, "The eyes aren't quite right," or "That thigh is too long," and Polyclitus would incorporate their suggestions into his work. All the while, however, he kept the other statue a secret. Both works were completed at about the same time and were mounted in the city square in Athens. The statue that had been designed by committee was openly mocked and ridiculed. The statue he'd done by himself was immediately proclaimed a great transcendental work of art. People asked Polyclitus, "How can one statue be so good and the other so bad?" And Polyclitus answered, "Because *I* did this one and *you* did that one."

So what can you do if you don't have talent? To paraphrase Claytie Williams, you can relax and enjoy it. Any no-talent fat boy can make it to the top of the charts, but it takes real talent,

"My client objects to the endless delays in this trial. Attorney fees alone, he says, are becoming increasingly painful to bear."

like that of the brilliant American composer, Stephen Foster, to die penniless in a gutter on the Bowery. But with or without talent, you might ask, how can hard work and perseverance pay off in the creative field? Why are you asking me? Who the hell knows? In this day and age, just as the tortoise is finally crossing the finish line to win the race, he'll very likely see three men in suits and ties, standing there with their briefcases. "Hello," they'll say. "We're the attorneys for the hare."

STRANGE TIMES TO BE A JEW: NOTES ON MICHAEL CHABON'S LATEST NOVEL

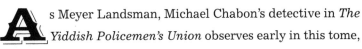

As Meyer Landsman, Michael Chabon's detective in *The Yiddish Policemen's Union* observes early in this tome, "These are strange times to be a Jew." Not one to flail the passive horse of Judaism forever, Chabon is merely intimating that down through history the times have never been quite as strange as the Jews. And one of the strangest of them all is, of course, Michael Chabon.

I'm sixty-two years old but I read at the sixty-four-year-old level. Nevertheless, at 432 pages, the book looked to me to be the kind of thing only a mother, and I use that word loosely, could love. Maybe a spiritual invalid might have the time, inclination, or reason to read it, I thought. Was it a great existential work of art or simply a case of *Northern Exposure* meets *The Emperor Has No Clothes*? Read on, gentile reader, read on.

When someone takes a simple idea and makes it complex, that is what we call an intellectual. When someone takes a complex idea and makes it simple, that is what we call an artist. Chabon assuredly is an intellectual, but is he an artist? Sherlock Holmes, whom Chabon professes to greatly admire, once observed that the difference between the killer and the artist is that the artist knows when to stop.

Great artists, in my reckoning, have always been out-of-control forces, invariably intertwining passionately their lives with their art. Examples are van Gogh, Mozart, Charles Bukowsky, Hank Williams, Edgar Allan Poe, Oscar Wilde, Stephen Foster, Allen Ginsberg, etc., etc. The fact that most of them were seen as tragic figures was no accident; it is merely one of the elements of their greatness. Bob Dylan once wrote that even above life, he prized madness. Contrast this with Chabon's almost primal pursuit of a "stable writing environment." Tell that to Franz Kafka.

But I suppose that I can overlook the fact that he's a script doctor for soulless *Spiderman* sequels and that he received a Pulitzer Prize from the same kind of crazy, tall Norwouija boards who gave the Nobel Peace Prize to Yasser Arafat and Jimmy Carter. Hell, my hat's off to him for just being able to write with four kids in the house.

Okay, so I'm reading *The Yiddish Policemen's Union* at gunpoint and I'm starting to like it. Chabon, with the lush skills of an F. Stop Fitzgerald, describing the deserted lobby of the flophouse hotel, the sad, old sofas and "ashtray charm," where Landsman has been living since his marriage went to hell. There's a "dead yid in 208," murdered during what appears to be a party-of-one chess match. So Chabon has his detective talk to the night manager about chess, Landsman admitting to having "no feel for the middle game." "In my experience, Detective," said the night manager, "it's all middle game." In spite of Chabon's unspoken, possibly unwitting, kinship with Flaubert, who claimed he lived to pour a few more buckets of shit upon mankind, this is great stuff.

If the slivovitz-swilling Landsman lives in a strange time, it is playing out in an even stranger place—the fictional Yiddish frontier district of Sitka, a Jewish homeland carved from Alaska after World War II. (Chabon borrowed the idea from a long-forgotten but real wartime proposal of FDR's.) The Palestine experiment failed early, in Chabon's telling, so in place of Sabras in the Jewish iconography, he offers "Polar Bears." Even lobs a sly dig at Israelis when he writes of the Sitkans, "By now they were all staunch Alaskan Jews, which meant they were utopians, which meant they saw imperfections everywhere they looked." Their temporary nation is nearing its sixty-year expiration date, and a new Jewish expulsion looms as the story opens.

In true noir fashion, "rogue cop" Landsman finds himself drawn irresistibly into pursuing whoever killed his chess-whiz neighbor, who turns out to have been a junkie and the son of a separatist Hasid rebbe. Also in true noir fashion, the higher-ups want him off the case. Landsman's investigation—in the company of his half-Tlingit, half-Jew partner—wraps him in the tassels of orthodox gangsters, international conspiracies about the impending "Reversion" of Sitka, and the allure of his sexy boss, who happens to be his ex-wife.

It's the easiest thing in the world to poke fun or parodize the field of detective fiction. Many highly successful mystery writers do it every day without even being aware of it. I respect Chabon for respecting the genre. Mysteries and mystery writers seem to have always been regarded by the critics as the stepchildren of literature. Yet here, in *The Yiddish Policemen's Union,* the timeless, glorious game is afoot: the reader ten steps ahead of the detective; the author ten steps ahead of the reader. On a truly seminal level, whether the critics notice it or not, *The Yiddish Policemen's Union* works as a mystery novel. There's a bit of John D. MacDonald here, a lingering hint of Dorothy Sayers. But in many ways the book is an homage to Raymond Chandler, who believed that plots were merely excuses for the characters to go places and say things.

Chabon clearly believes in the genre, as well he should. After all, mysteries afford us resolution; life itself rarely does. There's an obscure quote of Chandler's from one of his letters that I'm sure hasn't escaped detection by Chabon's micro-meticulous, mental hospital research. Chandler says, "The business of fiction is to recreate the illusion of life." Chabon does this as well as anybody.

Finally, J. D. Salinger once obliged a character to say, "Cleverness is my wooden leg." This may indeed be true of many writers and many Jews, but it's especially true of Chabon, who wears his yellow star on his wooden leg. This is not a bad thing.

It means Chabon is not an impotent, neurotic Woody Allen–Seinfeld-type of Jew, but a crazy Jew with all the elements of greatness who's never afraid to take a crack at the big dream. His Landsman is a brawler, a union man, toughing it out a continent and a world away from the skinny, self-loathing intellectuals who, when not writing, are busy in therapy sessions with Woody Allen's shrink.

Jackie Mason, whom I admire intensely, reports that older Jewish ladies come up to him after almost every show. Like reform harpies, they whisper in his ear, "Too Jewish. Too Jewish." Mason never listens to them. I hope Chabon doesn't either.

Oh, yeah. The more I read *The Yiddish Policemen's Union*, the more I believe I might finish it some day. Right now I'm reading it at almost a remedial pace, savoring it like an unfinished symphony. I'm even starting to like Chabon. If I ever run into him I'll have to tell him to take some of my critical comments with a pillar of salt. But then again, as Raymond Chandler himself once said, "If you like the book, never meet the author."

DON'T FORGET

In the dead of the night I started to write. If the editor wanted more pages, I'd give him more pages. If the agent wanted more action, I'd give her more action. But first, I felt it was necessary to write an homage to Clyde and Fox. As characters, I had them down cold by now, I thought, and certainly I could complete the novel out of my own imagination, which is what every reader would believe it to be anyway. I did not need any longer to faithfully chronicle their ridiculous little hobbies and adventures out of the whole cloth of their existence. They were characters and I was the author. I could make them do or say anything I wanted now. Maybe Clyde had been right all along. Maybe I was destroying them. What an odd occupation I had, I thought wryly. I was destroying them to create them. But it had to be done. And yet, I missed them. I realized, almost wistfully, that I might never see them again.

I started with Fox, hearing his voice in random past conversations, empathizing with his nuthouse background, getting inside his head. I felt like Faulkner, throwing the story to the winds. I felt like McMurtry, writing two hundred pages of boring shit before I really got going. I felt like J. D. Salinger, who only mixed interpersonally to get inside the heads of real people, then cut them out of his solitary life and nailed their hearts and souls to the page with a million typewriter keys. I felt like Fox and I felt crazy like a fox and I felt nothing. So, I said my farewells to Fox by writing a sort of soliloquy in his voice and putting him back in a mental hospital.

A mental hospital is not always as romantic a place as it's cracked up to be. You always think of Ezra Pound or Vincent van Gogh or Zelda Fitzgerald or Emily Dickinson or Sylvia Plath or someone like that. Not that all the above-mentioned people resided in mental hospitals. All of them probably belonged there, but so do most people who don't reside in mental hospitals. I know Emily Dickinson never went to a mental hospital, but that's just because she never went anywhere except, of course, for brief walks in her garden with her dog, Austin. If she'd ever gone into a mental hospital and talked to the shrinks for a while, they never would have let her out. She might've done some good work there but that would've been her zipcode for the rest of her life.

Now you take van Gogh, for example. He lived in one with a cat and did some good work there. They put him in for wearing lighted candles on his hat while painting "Night Café." Today, the arbiters of true greatness, Japanese insurance companies, have determined that his work is worth millions.

Sylvia Plath I don't know too much about except she wrote good prose and maybe some great poetry, and then she put her head in an oven and killed herself, but by then it was too late for her to reside in a mental hospital. Everybody thought she was crazy for many years until her husband's second wife also croaked herself and then people began to wonder if maybe Sylvia had been all right and it was her fucking husband who was crazy. I mean, to have two wives conk on you like that, I mean each one topping herself on your watch, pretty well indicated to most people outside of mental hospitals that if that husband wasn't crazy there was something wrong with him.

Now Ezra Pound I don't know a hell of a lot about except he hated Jews and still managed to do some pretty good work in wig city. Hitler and Gandhi, both of who probably belonged in wig city, for different reasons, no doubt, somehow managed to avoid the nuthouse circuit. They each did, however, spend a bit of time in prison, which in some ways is not as bad as being in a mental hospital except that you come out with an asshole the size of a walnut. In a sense Hitler and Gandhi, who may well represent polar opposites of the human spirit, each found himself in prison where the absence of freedom and the distance from their dreams may have contributed to their achieving some pretty good work. Hitler, who hated Jews almost as much as Ezra Pound, wrote *Mein Kampf*, which was almost immediately translated into about fourteen languages and would have made him quite a favorite at literary cocktail parties if he'd been willing to stop there.

Unfortunately, he couldn't hold a candle to Anne Frank. Gandhi, who spent his time in prison listening to a South African mob singing "We're gonna hang ol' Gandhi from a green apple tree," did some scribbling of his own but mostly realized that he was tired of London yuppie lawyer drag and it was time for visions and revisions both sartorially as well as spiritually. But God only knows how Hitler and Gandhi, who were both interesting customers, would have fared had they been incarcerated in mental hospitals instead of prison. As it was, each man found himself in prison, something that almost never happens in a mental hospital because shrinks are constantly prescribing meds that keep you invariably, perpetually, hopelessly lost. Speaking of lost, Zelda Fitzgerald certainly qualifies in that category and technically, I suppose, she was confined to a "sanitarium," which was not truly a mental hospital if you want to be a purist about it, but no doubt still probably had a sign in the lobby that read: THIS IS TUESDAY. THE NEXT MEAL IS LUNCH. She'd been drinking a lot of her meals evidently and so they'd put her in this sanitarium in Ashville, North Carolina, or maybe it was Ashville, South Carolina. I always get those two states mixed up. Where are the Wright Brothers when you need them?

Anyway, the irony of the whole situation was that the sanitarium was in Ashville and the place burned down one night with Zelda and a fairly good-sized number of other no-hopers inside. I've wondered why God so often seems to send fires and other catastrophes to sanitariums and mental hospitals. It's kind of like swerving to hit a school bus. But all that being as it may, it's just ironic, I thought, that the sanitarium burned down and that it was in Ashville. But before Zelda came along to screw things up I was commenting on the fact that mental hospitals are far more sad and sordid places than you'd think, seeing as all these colorful, fragile, famous, ascetic people populate them. I mean it isn't all van Gogh and his cat. I mean there are men following you with their penises shouting, "Am I being rude, mother?" in frightening falsetto voices. People in mental hospitals are shrieking like mynah birds all the time. Or masturbating.

Now Dylan Thomas was a good one. He used to masturbate a lot but I don't think they ever put him in a mental hospital, though God only knows he belonged there. And speaking of God only knows, Brian Wilson undoubtedly belongs there, too, except what would happen to the Beach Boys if you put Brian Wilson in the nuthouse? I mean the only one of those guys who was really a surfer was Dennis Wilson. And you know what happened to him? He drowned. Ah well, the channel swimmer always drowns in the bathtub, they say. But I suppose I've come pretty far afield in this tawdry little tale that the shrinks would assuredly call a rambling discourse. But if getting to the point is the determinant of whether or not you're crazy, then half the world's crazy. Trouble is it's the wrong half. I mean whoever said anything important by merely getting to the point? Did guys like Yeats and Shelly and Keats who, by the way, all belonged in mental hospitals, ever get to the point? I mean what's the point of getting to the point? To show some shrink with a three-inch dick that you're stable, coherent, and well grounded?

And I haven't even gotten to Jesus yet. Sooner or later everybody in a mental hospital gets around to Jesus, and it's a good

thing that they do because I'll let you in on a little secret: Jesus doesn't talk to football coaches. He doesn't talk to televangelists or Bible Belt politicians or good little churchworkers or Christian athletes or anybody else in this god-fearing, godforsaken world. The only people Jesus ever really talks to are people in mental hospitals. They try to tell us but we never believe them. Why don't we, for Christ's sake? What have we got to lose? Millions of people in mental hospitals who say they've talked to Jesus can't all be wrong. It's the poor devils outside of mental hospitals who are usually wrong or at least full of shit and that's probably why Jesus never talks to them. Anyway, you can probably tell by the fact that I'm not employing any paragraphs and the fact that I'm not employing any paragraphs and the fact that I'm not employing any paragraphs and the fact that this little rambling discourse tends to run on interminably that this looks like a mental hospital letter itself. If that's what you think, you're right, because I am in a fucking mental hospital as I'm writing this tissue of horseshit and it's not one of those with green sloping lawns in that area between Germany and France that I always forget the name of. Hey, wait a minute! It's coming to me. Come baby come baby come baby come. Alsace-Lorraine! That's where the really soulful mental hospitals are.

Unfortunately, I'm writing this from a mental hospital on the Mexican-Israeli border and I'm waiting for a major war to break out and they don't have any green sloping lawns. They don't even have any slopes. All they have is a lot of people who talk to Jesus, masturbate, and don't believe they belong in here. It's not a bad life, actually, once you get the hang of it, unless of course you hang yourself, which happens here occasionally, usually on a slow masturbation day. Anyway, the reason I'm telling you all this is that I really don't belong here. I've told the doctors. I've told the shrinks. I've even told a guy who thinks he's Napoleon. The guy's six foot tall, weighs two hundred and fifty pounds, and he's black, and he thinks he's Napoleon. I probably shouldn't have told him in the first place. But the funny thing is he's right. I don't belong here.

The other day a woman reporter came in here from the local newspaper to do some kind of exposé on the place and she interviewed some of the patients and one of them was me. I told her I was perfectly sane and I didn't belong in here. She asked me some questions and we chatted for a while and then she said that I sounded really lucid and normal to her and she agreed that I really didn't belong in here. Then she asked me since I seemed so normal what I was doing here in the first place and I told her I didn't know I just woke up one day and here I was and now the doctors won't let me out. She said for me not to worry. She said when she finished her exposé on my condition, these doctors would have to let me out. Then she shook my hand and headed for the door. About the time she turned to open it I took a Coke bottle and threw it real hard and hit her on the back of the head.

"Don't forget!" I shouted.

A TRIBUTE TO ME

Usually you have to be dead before famous musicians pay homage and record your songs. Did you really think I would wait?

God and country being what they are, you usually have to go to Jesus before anybody gives you a tribute album. The late Townes Van Zandt, who was the precise weight of Jesus at the time of his death, now has about ten of them. Jesus, of course, has more. But when Jesus was alive, He was relatively uncelebrated and totally broke. That is why, directly following the Last Supper, He told the waiter, "Separate checks, please." True greatness is rarely recognized when it walks among us. It almost always dies in the gutter or, occasionally, in the back of a 1952 Cadillac, as Hank Williams did. Talent is invariably its own reward. As Bob Dylan once told me, "When you die, they let you off the hook." The leopard of humanity never changes its spots.

I'd been thinking about a tribute album to myself for a long time, but I didn't want to have to die to get it. I didn't want to be too successful either. If you're too successful in life, you'll never get a tribute album. Someone like Garth Brooks, the anti-Hank, is so commercially viable that probably no one will remember his name by the time he wakes up in hell next to Oscar Wilde. And that's the way the Lord wants it. The Lord doesn't want people singing Garth Brooks songs to their grandchildren. He wants them to sing the songs of the guy who died in the back of the Cadillac, or the songs of Willie Nelson, or the songs of Stephen Foster, who died on the Bowery in New York City. Or, I decided, the songs of the Kinkster, which is why some of you are now holding in your hands *Pearls in the Snow: The Songs of Kinky Friedman.*

How exactly did that fine record—picked as a spotlight album of the week in December by *Billboard*—come to be? Glad you asked. In the early seventies, along with my band, the Texas Jewboys, I traveled the land annoying many Americans with songs like "The Ballad of Charles Whitman" and "They Ain't Makin' Jews Like Jesus Anymore." I thank the Lord we didn't have a big hit because instead of getting a tribute album, I'd be playing Disneyland with the Pips. About two decades later, once I had enough decent (or indecent) songs and my career had gone so far south that people thought I was dead or wished I was, I knew the time was right for a tribute to me.

The first thing I needed was a title. Every tribute record requires a classic-sounding, moderately pretentious title. Fortunately, I had a number of them. The top contenders were *Ridin' 'cross the Desert on a Horse with No Legs*, *Strummin' Along with Richard Kinky Big Dick Friedman*, *Come Home, Little Kinky*, and Don Imus's rather facetious suggestion, *Hillbilly Has-Beens Sing the Hideous Songs of Kinky Friedman*. The title eventually chosen came from a conversation I'd had in the eighties with my friend Timothy B. Mayer, who's since gone to Jesus himself. Tim was lamenting the fact that my more sensitive songs had been overshadowed by obnoxious, outrageous ones like "Ol' Ben Lucas (Had a Lotta Mucus)," which I wrote when I was eleven years old. Tim said that the best songs I'd written had been lost over the years like "pearls in the snow." He told me this when we were both out where the buses don't run on a snowy New Year's Eve on Martha's Vineyard and I was urinating on a house and shouting, "It's going to be a power year for the Kinkster." (It wasn't.)

Fast-forward ten years or so. I was in Nashville hanging out one night with seminal Music City deejay Captain Midnight and Kacey Jones, formerly the lead singer of Ethel and the Shameless Hussies, when Kacey asked, "Whatever happened to all those beautiful songs you wrote?"

Paraphrasing Sammy Allred, I answered, "Nuthin'."

"Well," she said in a voice fraught with irritating gentile optimism, "why don't we do something about that?"

"Why don't we just get a drink?" Midnight said. As fate would have it, we did both.

Since Hank Williams was working a package show with Johnny Horton and Faron Young, we decided that the best centerpiece for our aural table would be Willie Nelson. We sent Willie a dozen vintage Kinky songs from which he was to select one tune to record for us. We waited for the gestation period of the southern sperm whale, but nothing happened. When a tribute album gets off to this kind of a slow start, the honoree can often become somewhat dispirited. I thought that possibly my own precisely timed country music death might increase interest in the project.

Then I saw the light: If you want mankind to honor you, you've got to get off your ass. I called Lana Nelson, Willie's daughter, and Doug Holloway, Willie's illegitimate son, promised each of them two or three hundred dollars, and soon the wheels were turning. (To quote Sammy Allred again, "When Kinky offers you two or three hundred dollars, you always know which one it's going to be.") Lana and Doug graciously refused the cash, and two weeks later Willie was in the studio with his band, recording a brilliant version of "Ride 'em, Jewboy." Later that night I sat in my car, listened to the cut, and smiled for the first time in two hundred years.

After Willie, we selected artists who, like him, walk their own roads. These were all people who, if someone in the record business said it couldn't be done, would spend the rest of their lives proving them wrong. Fortunately, they turned out to be the kind of stars a hopeful little Jewboy could make a wish upon. The only pain, disappointment, and humiliation I felt was when I was turned down flat by one particular person.

After all I've been through, I'm not reticent about mentioning that performer by name. The artist who rejected me was k.d. lang. I'd sent her my song "Get Your Biscuits in the Oven and Your Buns in the Bed." I still can't understand it.

As far as the actual recordings went, the artists chose their own song, studio, city, and planet. (We put the songs on the CD in the exact chronological order in which they were recorded; we didn't need the bungling hand of a record company mortal to play God.) Several of the songs were cut in Austin, but that didn't pose a problem, as I stayed the hell away. It's always a good idea for a songwriter to steer clear of the studio when someone is recording his song. On a tribute record, particularly, the honoree should be either dead or working in Branson— anywhere but lurking around the studio. I'm proud to say that I wasn't present for any of the fifteen guest-artist performances on *Pearls in the Snow*. Instead, I retired into a rather petulant snit, only emerging two years later, when everything was completed. I left the recording duties in the much more capable hands of Kacey, who served as supervising producer and turned out to be a pretty fair engineer as well. Of course, with a name like Kacey Jones, I was not all that surprised.

Money was an issue, of course. You've got to have money to make your own tribute album. If you're dead, you probably don't have any and the project moves along without you (or dies with you). If you're alive, the musicians and studio personnel, despite their obvious affection for you, like to get paid. Cognizant of this, I went to see my friend Johnny Marks in San Antonio. Johnny coughed up some bucks and officially became our executive producer. The bucks lasted until Dwight Yoakam did forty-nine overdubs on "Rapid City, South Dakota." Now we had a problem. With Willie, Dwight, Delbert McClinton, Lee Roy Parnell, Asleep at the Wheel, and the Geezinslaw Brothers already recorded, we had everybody in the can but Prince Albert, yet we still had only half a tribute album. "Half a hero's better than no hero at all," I said to Kacey one afternoon. "Get out of the studio," she said, "and get more money."

With my artistic feelers hurt now that the artist in me had been overtaken by the loan shark, I proceeded to fat-arm my friend John McCall in Austin. John ponied up more bucks and officially became, along with Johnny, coexecutive producer of *Pearls in the Snow*. As time went by, I repeatedly assured both former friends that the album would definitely be a financial pleasure. At about the two-year point, I changed my tune slightly. "Money may buy you a fine dog," I advised them, "but only love can make it wag its tail." This bit of folksy wisdom failed to comfort or amuse either man.

Nevertheless, McCall's money carried us through Guy Clark, Marty Stuart, Tompall Glaser, Chuck E. Weiss and the G-d Damn Liars, Billy Swan, Lyle Lovett, a rather triumphant if somewhat tedious reunion of the original Texas Jewboys, and Tom Waits. I don't know what studio Tom recorded his cut in, but you can hear roosters crowing in the background. This notwithstanding, his version of "Highway Café" remains one of my favorites. As Captain Midnight wrote in his liner notes, "If this music doesn't reach down and touch you, remember . . . it's only a fucking record."

The final responsibility I had before the CD was released was to obtain participation agreements from all the artists. It was a formality, but it had to be done, and as CEO of Kinkajou Records, it fell to me. (A kinkajou, by the way, is a cuddly little Central American mammal with a prehensile tail.) So it was, with contract in hand, that I accosted Willie Nelson on his golf course one fine afternoon late last summer. I'd drawn up the one-page contract myself, and if not entirely legally binding, it was at least a fairly humorous document. It concluded with the following statement: "Trust me. As a Jewish record company president, I will not fuck you."

Without hesitation, Willie graciously signed his name on the appropriate line. Underneath his signature, the greatest living country music star in the world today wrote, "Please fuck me."

But when all is said and done, every tribute album is really a tribute to all that has gone before. Just prior to *Pearls in the Snow* being released, I was playing a tape of it for Willie on his bus on the way to Gruene Hall, where he was doing a benefit for flood victims. Both of us were now straying rather dangerously off the reservation. We were listening to Lee Roy's poignant version of one of my earliest songs, "Nashville Casualty and Life."

"That sounds great," said Willie. "Sounds a lot like Merle."

"The influence wasn't Merle Haggard," I said. "Lee Roy told me that for two weeks before he went in the studio, he was listening to Lefty Frizzell."

"So was Merle," said Willie.

WHAT WOULD KINKY READ?

1. "The Murders in the Rue Morgue," by Edgar Allan Poe, 1843. This brilliantly tragic and peculiarly moral poet and author is widely regarded to have written the first, and certainly the most seminal, modern detective story. "The Murders in the Rue Morgue" has influenced generations of mystery writers all over the world for its pioneering demonstration of deductive reasoning.

2. "The Monkey's Paw," by W. W. Jacobs, 1845. Poe's great body of work and Robert Louis Stevenson's "Bottle Imp" notwithstanding, "The Monkey's Paw" may well be the most frightening, macabre, and downright spookiest story ever written. Always good to keep the night-light on for this one.

3. "A Study in Scarlet," by Arthur Conan Doyle, who first sent it off not very optimistically to *Strand* magazine in 1891. Conan Doyle's depiction of Sherlock Holmes and Dr. Watson is clearly the most celebrated latent homosexual relationship in all of literature. The Sherlock Holmes stories can be read many times in the same lifetime for their fog, friendship, and unique, oddly comforting flavor.

4. *A Pocket Full of Rye/The Mystery of the Blue Train,* by Agatha Christie. Though Hercule Poirot's head may be shaped like an egg, he is not Agatha Christie's greatest invention. Beyond question, that honor belongs to Miss Jane Marple, who divines great insights from the citizens of St. Mary Mead and applies these qualities to the world in general. Never underestimate Miss Marple.

5. *Busman's Honeymoon,* by Dorothy L. Sayers, 1937. Sayers is somewhat of a pointy-headed intellectual, perhaps, but her WASPY, dapper detective, Lord Peter Wimsey, is witty, eloquent, and fun. The books harken back to a more innocent, romantic era which, given our current spiritual ambience, is a welcome break.

6. *Maigret and the Headless Corpse,* by Georges Simenon, 1955. Simenon, who had every human weakness known to God and man, somehow managed to create a magnificently moral mender of destinies in the person of Inspector Maigret. This peerless series can be seen as a remarkable guide to the sometimes rather perverse study of human nature. Simenon wrote about seven million books, all beginning with the word "Maigret," and every one of them is killer bee.

7. *The Widows of Broome,* by Arthur W. Upfield. This Australian series features the half-aboriginal detective Napoleon Bonaparte who knows the outback better than Crocodile Dundee. These books are wild and weird and beautiful like the people and the country they describe. They offer sparkling insights into nature as well as human nature. Not to mention that *The Widows of Broome* is scary as hell.

8. *The Big Sleep,* by Raymond Chandler. Philip Marlowe, a spiritual pioneer in the American hard-boiled detective genre, is a man who walks his own road right through the middle of the mean streets of L.A.

Chandler once observed: "Scarcely anything in literature is worth a damn except what is written between the lines." He writes between the lines better than almost anyone before or since.

9. *The Green Ripper*, by John D. MacDonald. MacDonald's knight-out-of-time Travis McGee has become an enduring American hero. This stellar series reflects great compassion for human vulnerability, great sympathy for the ecology of this planet, and great empathy for the rare enough triumphs of love, justice, and life.

10. *The League of Frightened Men,* by Rex Stout. Nero Wolfe and Archie Goodwin are two of my all-time favorites. Like Chandler and MacDonald, (not to mention Jesus, van Gogh, and Emily Dickinson), Rex Stout was underappreciated in his day. Like every other author on this list, Stout is now a ranking member of the Dead Detective's Society, having many years ago stepped on a rainbow. Possibly because their creators have all checked out of this mortal motel, their fictional children seem more than ever alive today.

QUESTIONS FROM A BRITISH JOURNALIST — 1999

Can we start by talking about your latest book?

My latest book, entitled *Spanking Watson,* deals with my quest for the perfect Dr. Watson. It also deals rather extensively for the first time with the lesbian dance class in the loft above my own. It is at the same time more profound and more profane than my previous work. I leave it to the reader to determine what is profound and what is profane.

Who were the writers who inspired you in your fledgling efforts?

Well, it wasn't J. R. R. R. R. Tolkien, though I do admire the fact that he invented his own language and geography and was almost certainly clinically insane at the time of his best work. So were van Gogh, Emily Dickinson, and Jesus, of course. My early writing influences, however, were probably Simenon, Hank Williams, and Conan Doyle.

Is any of your early work publishable—or will it remain in a bottom drawer?

It was brilliant! And now it's lost to the ages! If I find any of that early shit I'll let you know. It probably is publishable. A lot of people are killing a lot of trees these days.

How do you regard your writing peers?

I belong to the Dead Poet's Society. Show me a book by a dead guy and it's probably going to be pretty good. Show me a book by a living human being and it's almost certain to be a dreary, derivative tissue of horseshit.

Violence and sexuality?

I don't do sex and violence very well so the point is kind of moot. I don't believe, however, in trying to protect people who hang themselves while masturbating: Who am I to try to stop them?

Tell me a little about your working methods?

When I write I pretend like I'm Oscar Wilde behind bars with my hair on fire. Also, you have to be pretty miserable to write humorous fiction that's worth a shit. The duller and more unhappy my life is, the sharper and funnier is my prose. So I fight happiness at every turn. I also strive not to be too successful in my lifetime. That's the kiss of death for immortality.

What do you feel is the principal appeal of the kind of fiction you write?

That would be hard to say. My life is a work of fiction. I'm merely writing an unauthorized autobiography over and over again. Hopefully, I'm getting a little better at it every time. But people are so perverse it's hard to imagine why they think something's funny. Especially Germans. I'm killing a lot of trees in the Black Forest these days. Maybe a few of them will fall on unsuspecting Germans.

Is music a factor in your inspiration?

As a former country singer and songwriter, my books are largely fueled, I believe, by the leftover lyrics of my life on the road. I wasn't that great a country singer but you have to fail at one thing before you can succeed at another. An eight-year-old who knew my situation, once asked me if I heard music in my head while I typed my novels. I told him yes. I thought it was a pretty insightful question for an eight-year-old. That kid will probably drive his car into a tree before he finishes high school. A lot of people are killing a lot of trees these days.

Do you remember a teacher or mentor who inspired you?

I had a few encouraging teachers along the way and I'm sure they've gone to Jesus by now and I don't really remember them too well. Miss Jean Brodie was pretty helpful. Of course, if you've taken as much Peruvian marching powder as I have, you're doing well to remember that today is Tuesday and the next meal's lunch.

Which comes first with you: plot or characters?

A plot can never come; only a character can. So I agree with George Bernard Shaw that plots are for cemeteries. I also agree with Raymond Chandler that plots are merely excuses for characters to go places and say things. Unfortunately, I don't agree with anybody else.

Is there a city that gets your creative juices flowing?

New York, of course. But the farther I'm away from it, the clearer it becomes in my mind. The characters become clearer too, the farther I get away from them. This includes myself, though it's rather difficult to get geographically away from yourself. It's not something you want to try at home. Anyway, it doesn't really work. A few weeks after you've gotten as far away as you can, you always see yourself in the rearview mirror.

How would you describe your relationship with your publisher and editor?

Not as friendly as Holmes and Watson, but not quite as latent homosexual.

Do you bear your potential reader in mind when writing or do you write for yourself?

If you keep the reader in mind you're an artistic whore. If you write for yourself you're a self-absorbed asshole. It's like trying to decide whether to kill yourself or go bowling. I suppose I write with an utter disregard, not to say a hard-on, for the reader, but this is not necessarily unhealthy.

Is reading important these days or a pleasant throwback to a vanishing past?

Reading is as important as ever. It's just that nothing else is. It's amazing how enduring some dead people's work really is. Oscar Wilde's "The Happy Prince," for example. It's kind of nice to know that a tortured homosexual can reach across an ocean and a century to touch a man and a cat.

Should a writer be of the world, or is a monastic solitariness useful at times?

I lead a lonely, ascetic, monastic lifestyle and it helps with my work. I don't like people anyway. They always look at me with pity in their eyes. I surround myself instead with animals and distance and croaked heroes who've crossed the rainbow bridge slightly ahead of the Kinkster.

Is the religious sense a help or hindrance for a writer?

I wouldn't know. I'm a Jehovah's Bystander. I think there might be a God but I don't want to get involved.

How do you feel about the fact that a writer is often a commodity, to be packaged and sold by a publisher?

A lot of people are killing a lot of trees these days.

What can you tell me about your next book?

It's entitled *The Mile High Club*. It's very similar to my last book except hopefully more profound and more profane. I'll leave it to the reader to determine which portions are profound and which are profane.

DOES NOT COMPUTE

ude, you're getting a Dell! You may be going to hell, but at least you'll be able to take your computer with you. You see, I believe the Internet is the work of Satan. As far as I can tell, this seductive spiderweb of insanity has only two possible functions. One is to connect a short, fat, sixty-five-year-old man in New Jersey who's pretending to be a tall, young Norwegian chap to a vice cop in San Diego who's pretending to be a fifteen-year-old girl. The other purpose of this international network is to establish, once and for all, who is everybody's favorite *Star Trek* captain.

Needless to say, I've never used the Internet, owned a computer, or had an e-mail address. Then again, why would anybody with a brain the size of a small Welsh mining town ever need those things? If you require information on a certain subject, go to one of those places, I forget what you call them, with a lot of books inside and two lions out front. Pick a title, sit on the steps, and read between the lions. This may seem like a rather Neanderthal method of education, but at least you won't be tempted to pretend to be someone you're not and you won't get carpal tunnel syndrome. In fact, the only things you're liable to get are a little bit of knowledge and some pigeon droppings on your coat—which most people will tell you, and most computers won't, means good luck.

Good luck, of course, is better than a good hard drive anytime. I'm not really sure what a hard drive is, but I've heard grownups speak of it in positive tones. I've always found it ridiculous to hear people talk about how expensive, sophisticated, fast, or small their computers are. There must be something Freudian here, but I don't know what it is. I'm sure Freud himself didn't know what a hard drive was since he'd never even been up to Amarillo.

Of course, one reason I don't use a computer is because I'm too much of a genius to learn how. In fact, I write on the last typewriter in Texas. I think that computers contribute to the homogenization of everyone's brain. The technological revolution is not bringing us closer together—it's merely making us more the same. I have this archaic idea that you should try to get it right the first time. And if you don't, you should tear out the page and throw it in the fire. If you know you can change everything with some kind of electronic mouse, you'll never know what it's like to fly without the magic feather. You'll never feel like Oscar Wilde behind bars with his hair on fire. Even Oscar had trouble with this sometimes. Maybe technology could have saved him. Maybe he could have called Emily Dickinson from a pay phone in the rain. Maybe Davy Crockett could have e-mailed Sylvia Plath from inside the Alamo, and she wouldn't have had to put her head inside the oven. But technology can't save everybody, and it may not be able to save anybody. There's no time between the windmill and the world to buy a van Gogh, help Mozart out of the gutter, Sharansky out of the gulag, Rosa out of the back of the bus, or Anne out of the attic.

The other night I got home from a rather extended road trip and found that lightning had struck the dish, which meant I couldn't watch *Matlock*. I figured I'd listen to a little music, maybe some Beethoven or Roger Miller. You can imagine my chagrin when I walked over and discovered that the cat had vomited on my CD player. Now I was forced to take the fifth on Beethoven. It was Roger and out. Without even the rudimentary elements of technological input in my life, I was truly back to the basics. There was nothing to do but think. Nothing to do but dream. Nothing to do but remember.

I recalled a small incident that had occurred earlier that afternoon when I'd walked into one of those OfficeMax places in Kerrville like a mad scientist, searching desperately for a cartridge that might mate harmoniously with the last typewriter in Texas. Of course, I didn't find it. As I was leaving in a snit, I saw an old-timer entering the place, carefully clutching what is now considered an antique, a hand-levered calculator. He was a tiny man with a long white beard and a crushed straw hat on his wizened head. He wasn't getting a Dell. He was just hoping that the young techno wizards at OfficeMax could repair his calculator.

"It's not even in the catalog!" the tall, impossibly young salesman crowed almost joyously. Other employees crowded around to voice similar expressions of amazement bordering upon ridicule over this piece of machinery that had once been a workhorse of American business. "This belongs in a museum!" they laughed. But it wasn't a museum piece to the old man, who carried it protectively out into the parking lot. I looked up at the garish chain store in the ugly strip mall in the little town that was growing increasingly similar to every other town. Something there is that doesn't love a mall, I thought. Something.

Back at the house that night, with the cat vomit slowly drying on the CD player, I sat back and lit up a cigar. I blew a smoke ring. It wasn't perfect, but it wasn't bad. I remembered how my old pal Wavy Gravy used to salute mistakes and imperfections. He said that's what made us human. Meanwhile, that obnoxious kid was back on TV, smiling satanically at me like some adolescent Ronald Reagan pitchman, telling me I'm getting a Dell. I don't want a Dell. I just want a typewriter cartridge. And the next time that kid says, "Dude, you're getting a Dell," I want a windmill to fall on him.

PART IV

ADVICE ON
GOING ON A
JOURNEY

TEXAS FOR DUMMIES

A ll my adult life I've been in the practice of giving advice to people who are happier than I am. I'm sure, like most born-again Texans, you're probably thrilled right now about moving here. Oh, you've no doubt heard stories about the wide-open spaces being mostly between people's ears, but you didn't believe them. Now, the prospect of being a Texan may make you happier than 95 percent of all dentists in America, but that doesn't mean you're going to fit in. Remember, happiness, like Texas, is a highly transitory state.

But maybe you've really set your ears back, and you're hell-bent on becoming a real Texan like John Wayne, who was from Iowa, or George Walker Bush, who is from Connecticut, or Molly Ivins, who is from California, or Jerry Jeff Walker, who is from New York. In that case, the least you can do is follow these few simple rules of the road for all modern Bubbas and Bubbettes. This, my fine-feathered foreign friend, is friendly advice, freely given. Follow it—or get the death penalty.

1. Get you some brontosaurus-foreskin boots and a big ol' cowboy hat. Always remember, only two kinds of people can get away with wearing their hats indoors: cowboys and Jews. Try to be one of them.

2. Get your hair fixed right. If you're male, cut it into a "mullet" (short on the sides and top, long in the back—think Billy Ray Cyrus). Or you can leave it long on top and cut it short on the sides and back. When you take off your cowboy hat, you'll have what I like to refer to as the Lyle Lovett Starter Kit. If you're female, make it as big as possible, with lots of teasing and hair spray. If you can hide a buck knife in there, you're ready. Grooming tip: If you can't find curlers big enough, use empty Dr Pepper cans.

3. Don't make the most common mistake all non-Texans make when they come down here—confusing Amarillo with the armadillo. Amarillo is a town in the Panhandle full of people who don't like being mistaken for armadillos. They're very conservative politically. The armadillo is a gentle creature. It tends to be much more middle of the road.

4. Buy you a big ol' pickup truck or a Cadillac. I myself drive a Yom Kippur Clipper. That's a Jewish Cadillac—stops on a dime and picks it up.

5. Just because you can drive on snow and ice where you come from does not mean you can drive in a Texas downpour. When it rains hard, stay home. If you have to drive, get on the highway, move into the fast lane, and go no faster than thirty-five miles per hour. If you have to drive at night, watch out for the deer. Only hit the ones with huge antlers because they make the best wall hangings. Christmas gift tip: Make you a nice fur coat with antlers and give it to your mother-in-law.

6. Don't be surprised to find small plastic bags of giant dill pickles in local convenience stores.

7. If you hear a redneck exclaim, "Hey, y'all, watch this!" stay out of his way. These are likely the last words he will ever say.

8. Remember: "Y'all" is singular, "all y'all" is plural, and "all y'all's" is plural possessive.

9. Texans have a strange way of talking. Get used to it. In my experience, I've always heard the word "Jewish" pronounced with only one syllable, such as, "He's Juush." When they pronounce the word "Jew," of course, it's invariably with about eleven syllables. An example of this would be: "She married a Jeeeeeeeee-wwwwwwwww!"

10. Don't call it "soda" or "pop." It's all Coke unless it's Dr Pepper.

11. Don't pet the dog standing in the back of the pickup no matter how small or how cute. All truck dogs are dangerous weapons. But a dog that is not in the back of a pickup is another story. We Texans love our dogs.

Like we always say: "Money may buy you a fine dog, but only love can make it wag its tail."

12. It is now legal to carry a concealed weapon in Texas. As a result, crime has gone down. An unfortunate side effect, however, is that there are now about 18 million ambulatory time bombs any place you go just waiting for Dustin Hoffman to pound on the hood and shout, "I'm walkin' here!" As for myself, I don't carry a weapon. If anybody wants to kill me, he's going to have to remember to bring his own gun.

13. Everything goes better with picante sauce. No exceptions.

14. Be sure you have a favorite football team. Be sure it is the Dallas Cowboys.

15. Don't tell us how you did it up there. Nobody cares.

NEVER TRAVEL WITH
AN ADULT CHILD

Robert Louis Stevenson once said: "To travel hopefully is a better thing than to arrive." This is particularly true, of course, if you've lost your luggage. In the fall of 1985, realizing that it's sometimes best to leave life's excess baggage behind, my father and I finally agreed upon something. We decided to take a trip together to Australia.

Our publicly stated purpose was to put to rest once and for all two eternally vexing questions that have troubled mankind down through the centuries: Does water swirl counterclockwise in Australian toilets? And do Australian dogs circle counterclockwise three times before flopping down in the dust? Possibly a phone call to friends in Sydney might've helped resolve these matters, but, like all hopeful travelers, we wanted to find out for ourselves.

It is never highly recommended for a father and his child to travel together upon such an extensive journey, particularly if the child is almost forty-two years old and both father and son derive from a small, ill-tempered family. If indeed this is the case, human buffers are definitely in order to keep a peaceful pilgrimage from boomeranging into a rather repellent tension convention.

When you ask people if they'd like to go to Australia, they invariably tell you it's the dream of their lives. They'd love to go, they all say, but, fortunately for Australia, most of them never do. They cling perversely to that tar baby that is the quiet desperation of their lives. If they have the time, they don't have the money. If they have the money, they can't spare the

time. Few of the folks we talked to realized that time is the money of love. What they *did* realize, apparently, was that traveling halfway around the world with Dr. Tom Friedman and his son, Kinky Friedman, could make for an extremely unpleasant experience.

After searching the American countryside high and low, Tom and I at last came upon two brave souls who stood ready to accompany us on our father-and-son odyssey. One was Earl Buckelew, an old-time rancher and neighbor of ours who hadn't been outside of Medina, Texas, in more than fifty years. Earl was old enough to be a member of the Shalom Retirement Village People, but youthful in spirit and more vigorous than many men younger than he, Tom and myself included. Earl was one of the last real cowboys I've ever known.

The other candidate for the journey was my longtime journalist friend from New York, Mike McGovern. McGovern was a large half–Native American, half–Irish legend who rarely had much trouble getting into trouble. He was, however, not without charm. McGovern, reportedly, had once combed his hair before meeting a racehorse. Taken together, I'd always felt that McGovern and I just about comprised one adequate human being.

The four of us taken together, however, comprised a new, rather reckless, dangerously unstable entity. McGovern, ever the adept headline writer, dubbed our little troupe The Four Horsemen of the Antipodes. Earl did not know what the Antipodes were, but he was beyond doubt the only one of us who could really ride a horse. I preferred two-legged animals and I myself wasn't entirely sure what the Antipodes were, either. McGovern told me to look it up when I got home, but I soon discovered the meaning when I found myself in the outback riding 'cross the desert on a horse with no legs.

The flight to Australia takes just a trifle longer than the gestation period of the giant sea turtle, but there are always at least three full-length movies to divert the passengers. After each movie, Earl Buckelew, still wearing his cowboy hat, asked the flight attendants, whom he consistently called stewardess, whether they were male or female, how much time was left in the flight. Every time he asked, it seemed they always gave him the same answer: "About eight and a half hours."

A flight of this length gives you a chance to get to know yourself and your companions a bit more than you might've wished, but somehow we managed. My biggest problem was a satanic little baby sitting directly behind us who kept deliberately sneezing upon me. Tom's road-to-Damascus experience came when he learned that through some mix-up all that was left for his lunch was a vegetarian meal. He promptly became highly *agitato,* but I'm pleased to report that he did settle down after about eight and a half hours. "This is *exactly* what I didn't want to happen," he told the mother of the small infant behind us, whereupon the child maliciously sneezed upon me again.

McGovern made do with many little bottles of vodka, teaching the flight attendants and other privileged passengers how to make a rather arcane drink called a Vodka McGovern. By the time we crossed the international date line, he was so high he was starting to get lonely. I was cookin' on another planet myself. Earl captivated almost everyone he talked to and he never stopped talking once we left the States. They'd never met a real Texan before, one who'd driven an actual horse-and-wagon, sheared sheep, broken wild horses, built houses with his own hands, and especially one whose own grandfather had been captured by the Comanches. It was a good thing Earl was delighting these people, I thought, because I had pretty well run out of charm, and the baby behind me was now locked in a terrible rictus of unpleasant hiccupping. As for McGovern, he was singing "Waltzing Matilda" with a nun from Syracuse, New York. As they tell you down under: "No worries, mate."

It's probably just as well that the images of our first days in Australia, having percolated within my gray-matter department for many years, seem now as only bright pieces of a mosaic in my mind. Even when you're there, there is a faraway, ephemeral, *On the Beach*-like quality to Australia that has nothing to do with how heavily monstered you are when you arrive. It's something you see embodied in ancient Aboriginal paintings, all of which were created with a series of dots of color. You can see these paintings in some Sydney gallery, but when you fly over the outback and look down at the landscape, it is precisely and uncannily similar in style and detail to the Aboriginal art. Back when the paintings were made, of course, no Aboriginal had ever flown in an airplane. In fact, the first person to ever fly an airplane in Australia was an American—Harry Houdini. And about the only feat Houdini never attempted, as far as we know, was to draw Aboriginal paintings.

Houdini, however, would definitely not have been challenged by the old hotel we stayed at that first week in Townsville on the Gold Coast. There were no locks on any of the doors. The hotel was a sprawling affair that looked like an old set from "Gunsmoke," with a pub downstairs and a wide veranda encircling the entire structure. Tom and Earl shared the singular honor of having the only room in the place with a bathtub and toilet. I asked Tom whether he would mind monitoring whether the water swirled counterclockwise in the toilet, but, for the moment, he did not seem entirely committed to the project.

Later that night, down in the open-air pub with drunken Aussies throwing darts across the bridges of our noses, McGovern and I were drinking Cascade beer from Tassie (Tasmania) and listening to a British tourist bellyaching about his bad luck. He'd hit a kangaroo in his Land Rover and, not wanting to miss a photo op for the folks back home, had taken the dead body, dressed it up in his jacket, knapsack, and sunglasses, and leaned it against a nearby gum tree. He was taking the kangaroo's photo when the animal, apparently only stunned, suddenly bounded away with all his money and his passport.

"Now I'm stuck here broke and getting bitten to death by the bloody flies," he complained.

"Serves you right, mate," said one of the locals. "First you run down one of our 'roos. Next thing, you'll be swattin' our flies."

Before our daunting journey into the vaunted outback, the Four Horsemen spent a few relaxing days sailing on a forty-two-foot yacht along the Great Barrier Reef. Our hosts, Piers and Suzanne Akerman, were both excellent sailors, which made up for McGovern and myself, who spent most of our time pouring large amounts of Mount Gay rum down our necks and spitting up on the vessel's rather ornate brass compass. At night we watched the Southern Cross, the most beautiful of constellations, roll from one side of the cathedral sky to the other. "Makes you wonder," said McGovern, "what God might've done if He'd had a little money."

At one point, we dropped anchor and went ashore onto Hamilton Island, considered to be one of the most exclusive travel destinations in the world. Not only did we feed kookaburras by hand, we saw many animals that neither Dr. Seuss nor Earl Buckelew had ever dreamed of. There also appeared, however, to be another kind of animal—a fairly large herd of American businessmen. Tom Friedman confessed to being mildly disappointed. "We've come halfway round the world to this fabled, exotic island," he said, "only to discover an Amway convention."

Several days later, our gutsy little group set out on a secular pilgrimage to the outback. We had three major objectives in undertaking the trek. One was to prove we could do it. Two was to develop a firsthand understanding of the aboriginal culture. Three was to get the hell away from the Amway convention.

In my twin roles as Virgil leading Dante into the concentric circles of hell, and as official biographer for the Four Horsemen (which was far more tedious), I devised a helpful little list of things a tourist would require to make the trip safely. I also included a list of items an Aborigine would require making the same trip. As an educational service to the reader, the two lists are provided forthwith.

The tourist needs the following things to survive in the outback: sturdy hiking boots, large canteen with emergency supply of fresh water, first-aid kit, two-way radio, flashlight, tinned foods of every variety under the sun (that's why they need to be tinned), broad-brimmed hat with hole punched in one side of the brim for two-way-radio or walkie-talkie antennae, gun and knife for protection in case you meet someone as crazy as yourself, current map of the area (though nothing's changed since Banjo Paterson wrote the lyrics to "Waltzing Matilda" in 1895), and emergency phone and fax numbers so that you can contact the nearest koala bear with a pager (though, of course, they're not really bears), and antisnake and antispider venom, (though if you're bitten by the redback spider it's curtains on opening night). The female redback eats her mate, incidentally, during mating. The male redback, according to Piers Akerman, has a corkscrewlike procreative device. This may account for the female redback's behavior.

If you're bitten by the taipan snake, I'm afraid there won't be time to upgrade your software. The taipan denatures the blood, breaking it down totally and instantaneously. The taipan, the Aussies say, can kill a horse in half a second. That concludes the list of items the tourist needs to survive in the outback.

The Aborigine's list of necessities is much shorter, of course. In fact, it contains only one item: a stick.

With that same stick, we watched an Aborigine dig up several white larval grubs from under the red dirt of the desert.

How he knew where to find them is a mystery locked in past and future Aboriginal history, or Dreamtime, as they call it. He popped the thing live into his mouth, placing it headfirst on the back of his tongue so when he swallowed it would crawl downward and not back up.

"We call this witchity grub," he said, offering the sickly white, wriggling object to the Four Horsemen.

We looked at the grub and, I suppose, it looked at us. Tom had been a highly decorated flying hero in World War II. McGovern had been a Marine and had ingested many strange things in his life. I'd been in the Peace Corps in Borneo and had once eaten monkey brains. But it was Earl Buckelew, a man who'd never heard of sushi, who was finally brave enough to take the bait, so to speak.

"Care for an after-dinner mint?" I asked him later.

"You know," he said, "it's one of the few things I've eaten in my life that damn sure doesn't taste like chicken."

In the days ahead, we saw many strange animals and people and did many strange things. We survived climbing Ayers Rock, sacred to the Aborigines (thirty-five climbers at this count have died trying). We saw the famous black swans of Perth. McGovern almost got pecked by a poison parakeet near Darwin. Earl entered and won a sheep-shearing contest in New South Wales. I explored the area where the great Breaker Morant and his horse, Cavalier, had once happily wandered before the Boer War. Tom questioned the authenticity of a cannon that Piers Akerman claimed "fired the first shots in anger in both world wars, Australia being sixteen hours ahead of Texas and probably lightyears ahead of Sarajevo where Archduke Ferdinand was assassinated." By the time he'd gotten to how the cannon had started World War II by firing upon a German merchant vessel, the Four Horsemen had cantered off to the nearby town of Robertson, where the movie *Babe* was filmed many years later.

If you go there today and ask for Babe, you'll find that they are tired of fielding questions about their local celebrity. They'll probably tell you, "Sorry, mate. Babe's touring America. He's opening for David Helfgott."

For a country that's roughly the same size as the United States, with only eighteen million people and thirty million kangaroos, both groups of whom happily hop about in the sunshine away from the world's problems, Australia can't be beat. As a vacation paradise, the Four Horsemen give it four stars, one for every star in the Southern Cross.

But as far as questions about whether the water swirls counterclockwise in toilets or whether dogs circle three times counterclockwise before lying down, I'm afraid you'll have to travel down under yourself to find out. I know, of course, but I can't give you the answers. The Four Horsemen of the Antipodes have taken a sacred, eternal, monastic vow to carry them with us into Dreamtime.

HOW TO DELIVER THE PERFECT AIR KISS

What is an Air Kiss?

The air kiss, long the domain of vapid starlets and anorexic models, has made its way into mainstream America with a loud "muwah!" While the air kiss may seem to be a phenomena of the twenty-first century, the term was actually coined in 1887 in an article from the *Chicago Tribune* that described various forms of kissing: "Nothing is more dainty than the kiss of a well-bred chaperon, who, mindful of the time and trouble spent over the powder box, gently presses her lips on your hair just north of your ear. The minister's wife is another sweet soul who knows where a kiss will do least harm, and her favorite method is an air kiss, with the gentle pressure of her cheek to your cheek."

The air kiss no doubt remained in American culture but the term didn't reappear in print again until *Newsweek,* March 1975: "The uncontested Prince of American Design murmured greetings to the chic crowd, carefully air-kissing their cheeks."

Air kisses are most common in formal social occasions, such as weddings, official ceremonies, or celebrity parties where you have to mingle and pretend to feel care and affection for people you barely know and probably hate. There are a series of important steps you have to make in order to deliver an effective air kiss, and if you follow my guide, in no time you will be an expert at displaying pseudo affection and reassuring people of the sincerity of your pretension.

The Approach: Greeting people with an actual kiss can spread disease and give the false impression that you're actually happy to see them. If you sense that another person is about to plant one on you, launch a preemptive air kiss attack: spread your arms wide, tilting them slightly at an angle, and announce the person's name loudly. If you don't remember their name, say, "Look at yeww!" If you're in Texas, the "look at yeww!" will be reciprocated and elongated as "Look at ye-wwwww!"

The Ready Position: Move in and grasp the other person's hands, clutching them to your chest. This makes you look friendly and it also puts up a barrier between you and the other person without making you look like an antisocial ass. Air kissing is all about false impressions so you might as well use it to make yourself look good. Tilt your head slightly and move your right cheek next to their right cheek, but don't actually touch them. If they try to abort the air kiss to turn it into a real kiss, tighten your grip on their hands and don't let them pull away or alter the cheek position. If you allow them to parry the air kiss and turn it into an actual kiss, you will be doomed to greet-kiss this person forever. When you decide to air kiss, you have to be resolute and stay the course.

The Pucker: Now that your cheek is next to their cheek, pucker your lips firmly. Visualize yourself as a suckerfish clinging to the gills of a great white shark. Your lips must be firm and unforgiving; if you allow any softness at all, your air kiss might be mistaken for a Euro air kiss, which lacks the insincerity of the American air kiss.

The Delivery: Kiss the air next to the other person's head. A loud, enthusiastic "muwah!" should accompany the kiss. You could also make cutesy kissing sounds but this isn't recommended if there are dogs nearby because *you* don't even want to be there, so why subject an innocent animal to a place that requires air kisses?

The Kiss: Always air kiss both sides of a person's face. A one-sided air kiss confuses everyone and might set you up for an embarrassing collision when the other person automatically goes for the second kiss and you stay where you are. A rapid succession of four, or even six air kisses should be saved for special occasions, like when a lot of important people are watching. They will think you learned that while vacationing abroad and you'll come across as quaint, even charming.

The Closer: Once you've completed your air kiss, immediately let go of the other person's hands and step-slide backwards. Pretend to see someone you know in the distance and give a little wave in their imaginary direction. Smile at the one you just air kissed and make the "call me" gesture before you move away decisively.

LET SAIGONS
BE BYGONES

———————— ◆ ————————

Thirty-five years ago, I refused to let my government send me to Vietnam. So why did I finally go? Because my kid sister asked me to.

Another answer to that good question is that Vietnam was a bad war. In the late sixties I'd been in the Peace Corps in Borneo helping people who wore conical hats and worked with water buffalo in rice paddies. When I returned to the good ol' USA, I found myself in the basement thinkin' 'bout the government. They wanted to send me back over to Asia to kill the same people. It was unconscionable, I told them. It wasn't even cost-effective. Neither argument, however, seemed to cut much ice with the draft board. I had to trot out a phalanx of rabbis and shrinks to confirm my insanity and thereby, perhaps quite literally, dodge the bullet.

But that was then and this is now. People in both the East and the West long ago decided to let Saigons be bygones. My own kid sister is currently, in fact, the head of the American Red Cross in Vietnam. Marcie has been based in Hanoi for several years and is in love with the culture and the people. "You won't believe it," she told me. "It's a country of eighty million people with no Christians, no Jews, no Muslims, no Starbucks, no McDonald's, and no Burger Kings. It's paradise!" So a few months ago I went to Vietnam to visit her. And guess what? She wasn't wrong.

Vietnam is halfway around the world from the sign in front of the Kerrville church that used to read "Jesus Is Our Quarterback." If you travel west you can get to the East in roughly twenty-four hours. That gave me a lot of time to think about Marcie, who's sixteen years younger than I, though we've always been close. I've watched with pride as she's developed into what she humorously refers to as a "professional do-gooder." She grew up in Austin, attended Yale and Berkeley, and came within a tadpole of being a Ph.D. in biology before jumping species and deciding to devote her efforts to that most troublesome and needy of all living creatures, the human being.

Soon Marcie was heading up disaster-relief teams in Nicaragua, after torrential flooding; in Kauai, after Hurricane Iniki; and in Turkey, after a series of devastating earthquakes. She has traveled and lived in places like China, Mexico, Australia, and Easter Island. Marcie also spent several years in Washington as a senior program manager at the Red Cross and seven summers directing our family's summer camp, Echo Hill

Ranch, with our father. By the time I visited her in Hanoi, she already had a large, colorful group of friends and colleagues. I didn't have to make new friends; I just borrowed hers.

One friend, Professor Nguyen Trong Nhan, a former Vietnamese minister of health, grew up watching old Hollywood cowboy movies. He said it had broken his heart to know that the American cowboy was fighting on the other side. Another friend, Larry Holtzman, had been a Peace Corps volunteer in Liberia when JFK was assassinated and was now busy dispensing contraceptives throughout Vietnam. I told him it was probably an easier gig than it would be in the States. "One nation under what's-his-name?" he said. Dr. Le Cao Dai had been a legendary Viet Cong hospital commander. His name has many meanings, depending on inflection and tonality; thus it was that a Swedish social worker followed the revered man around for seven years calling him Dr. Urine. Mr. Phan Thanh Hai works for the Danang Red Cross. When Marcie and I saw signs everywhere that read "March 29," we asked Mr. Hai what was up. Merely stating historical fact, he said, "That's the day we defeated the running dogs of American imperialism." Then there was Marcie's friend who owned a sugar factory and named his small boy Ice Cream.

The children of Vietnam are among the most attractive and charming in the world. They are bright, friendly, and inquisitive, and they often call out to American strangers like shy little birds singing, "Hen-no," which, of course, is how they pronounce "hello." Marcie has a special bond with these children: She recently helped procure, through the U.S. Department of

Agriculture, an eight-million-dollar soy milk program for the country's schools—the largest American Red Cross package of its kind in Southeast Asia.

Hanoi itself is a magical, ancient city currently inhabited by three million people, three million cell phones, and three million motorbikes. Throw some cars, bicycles, and rickshaws into the soup, and crossing the street becomes a Zen exercise. There are almost no traffic lights, signals, or lanes, so you must walk very slowly and confidently, allowing the motorbikes to zip by from both directions on either side of you. Whatever you do, once you've committed to crossing the street, you mustn't stop. If you freeze in the middle, they can't tell which way you're going to jump.

The Vietnamese people are intelligent, kindhearted, and industrious and, as Marcie says, "the very last people on earth with whom we should have gone to war." The Vietnamese like Americans; we are merely a footnote in their long history. They don't seem to carry grudges, even when perhaps they should— e.g., Agent Orange. I walked with Marcie on China Beach, in Danang, a long, lovely, nearly deserted stretch of sandy, scenic shoreline. It was hard to believe that the three hundred thousand American GIs who had once been garrisoned here had left almost no footprints in the sand. (For a brief time, Marcie thought about putting a message on the answering machine at her office saying, "Welcome to the American Red Cross office in Hanoi. We apologize for our thirty-year disruption in service.")

As I left Vietnam, oddly enough, I thought of the cheerful taxi driver who'd taken me to the Honolulu airport for the flight over. She'd been born in Saigon, and she'd never been to Hanoi. But her father had spent twenty years there in a re-education camp after the war. As a child she'd drifted with the boat people on a horrifying journey to Malaysia, the Philippines, and finally, Hawaii. Did she like it here? I asked. "I love America," she said.

So it is with all wars: Some will die, some will be heroes, some will be liberated, and some are still not free. The only thing we can be sure of is that nobody ever really wins.

WILD MAN
FROM BORNEO

Many years ago, in a faraway kingdom called The Sixties, when doctors drove Buicks and ecstasy couldn't be bought, there lived a man named John F. Kennedy. One day he stood on the lawn of the White House, pointed at a group of ragtag young Peace Corps volunteers, and said, "You are important people." And, indeed, time has proven the wisdom of his words. Forty-one years and more than one hundred countries later, the Peace Corps is a shining example of Americans working for the good of the world.

Little did I realize in 1965, as I drank coffee at the Night Hawk restaurant on the Drag in Austin and contemplated joining the late JFK's dream team, that I would soon be eating monkey brains in the jungles of Borneo. At the time, I was a

Plan II major at the University of Texas. There was nothing practical about graduating with a degree in Plan II. About all you could do with it was leave town with the carnival or join the Peace Corps. After much soul-searching, I opted for the one that would look best on my résumé.

I soon found myself in Syracuse, New York, in about twelve feet of snow, in Peace Corps training. My only friend was a guy named Willard who smoked nonfiltered Camels and, during the first night's mixer, promptly ran out onto the dance floor and bit a woman on the left buttock. Since these were the good old days before political correctness, Willard was not sent home ("deselected" was the term then in use) and went on to distinguish himself setting up a law school in Africa.

I did not fare quite as well as Willard, however. As part of my training, the Peace Corps sent me on a two-week "cultural

empathy" junket to Shady Rill, Vermont, where I lived with a family so poor that they brushed their teeth with steel wool. After returning to Syracuse, I learned Swahili and was interrogated at great length by Gary Gappert, a supercilious, pipe-smoking psychologist who felt that I might not be fully committed to the goals of the Peace Corps because I had a band back in Texas called King Arthur and the Carrots. Soon, much to my chagrin, I was the one the Peace Corps had chosen to be deselected.

I traveled about the country like a rambling hunchback, hitchhiking from place to place, singing Bob Dylan songs at truck stops. The truckers were not pleased. They enjoyed my behavior only marginally more than Gary Gappert had. Yet I had not abandoned my dream, and eventually I landed at another Peace Corps training program, this time in Hilo, Hawaii, where I was, at long last, hailed as a golden boy. It was also where I learned Malay, a language I can now speak only when I'm walking on my knuckles.

Ultimately I was sent to Borneo, where I wore a sarong, built compost heaps, and earned eleven cents an hour as an agricultural extension worker. My job was to teach people how to keep their heaps from falling over on top of the Kinkster. Somehow I managed to avoid the fate of one of my coworkers, who had to be airlifted out of his hut and back to the States by a shrink in a helicopter.

By the time Martin Luther King and Bobby Kennedy had been assassinated, I'd gone native. I'd taken to spending a lot of time at a Kayan longhouse fairly deep in the *ulu,* or jungle, up the Baram River from the little town of Long Lama. The Kayans were a spiritual people, but they were also rather serious party animals. They had a traditional combo that might have even been stronger than a John Belushi cocktail. It called for chewing betel nut until your lips turned blood red, smoking an unidentifiable herbal product in a jungle cigar, and then drinking a highly potent homemade rice wine called *tuak* that would have made George Jones jealous. The Kayans, like a tribe of persistent mother hens, would push this combination on every guest, and it was considered extremely bad form to turn down their offering. Accepting their largesse, however, would invariably lead to projectile vomiting. The Kayans had no perceptible plumbing, of course, so you'd simply vomit through the bamboo slits of the porch, or *ruai*. If, after being sick, you continued drinking tuak with them, the Kayans considered you a man and, even more important, a friend. The only time the Kayans found my behavior socially unacceptable was once when, after an extended harvest celebration, I accidentally vomited on the chief.

As a Peace Corps volunteer, my mission was to preserve the culture as much as possible while attempting to distribute seeds downriver. In two and a half years the Peace Corps failed to send me any seeds, so I was eventually reduced to distributing my own seed downriver, which led to some rather unpleasant reverberations. I was well aware that the Kayans, though now a gentle people, had once been headhunters, and I did not want an atavistic moment to occur in which my skull might take its place along with dozens of others in the hanging baskets that festooned the ruai. But while I supported the indigenous culture, the missionaries were constantly at work to destroy it. They encouraged the Kayans to cut off their long hair, throw away their hand-carved beads, and dance around the fire singing "Oh! Susanna." I've got nothing against "Oh! Susanna"—only against the missionaries who told the people to bow their heads and pray long enough so that when they looked up, their traditions were gone.

In a few short years, I was gone too. But all Peace Corps volunteers keep a little town or a little tribe deep in their heart, though they may have left it many years ago and many miles away. I remember fishing at night by torchlight with the Kayans in the Baram River in a small wooden boat called a *prahu*. Everybody got drunk on tuak and had a great time, though the Kayans never caught any fish. Of course, that wasn't their intention. The Kayan word for "fishing," in fact, means "visiting the fish."

I also remember the coffee-colored river. It seemed to flow out of a childhood storybook, peaceful and familiar, continue its sluggish way beneath the moon and the stars and the tropical sun, and then pick up force and become that opaque uncontrollable thing roaring in your ears, blinding your eyes, rushing relentlessly round the bends of understanding, beyond the banks of imagination.

MAD COWBOY
DISEASE

In *The Innocents Abroad*, Mark Twain observed, "They spell it Vinci and pronounce it Vinchy; foreigners always spell better than they pronounce." Twain didn't mention it, but they also spell better than they smell. All in all, very little seems to have changed since his time. There's nothing like a trip across the old herring pond to make you glad that you live in the good ol' USA.

I knew that early March wasn't the best time to be a cowboy in Europe, yet I felt I had to honor a commitment I'd made to address an event in London with an unfortunate title: "Murder at Jewish Book Week." Everyone told me it was sheer idiocy to travel overseas with the triple threats of war, terror, and customs inspectors taking away my Cuban cigars. Yet, strangely, it wasn't courage that compelled me to go. It was simply that I was afraid at that late date to tell the lady I was canceling.

The flight was nine and a half hours long. It seemed as if almost every passenger besides myself was dressed in some form or other of Middle Eastern garb. One young man who spoke English was wearing a Muslim prayer cap and robe over a University of Texas sweatshirt. He told me there was really nothing to be concerned about. "You have gangsta chic," he explained. "We have terrorist chic." I found his calm analysis oddly comforting.

I was totally jet-lagged when I arrived at London's Gatwick Airport at 6:55 in the morning. My ride into town was arranged by Robert MacNeil of the old *MacNeil/Lehrer NewsHour*. The day before, I'd been filming a PBS show with Robert in Bandera and had warned him about crossing the busy streets of the little cowboy town. "It'd seem quite ridiculous," I'd told him, "for a cosmopolitan figure like yourself to get run over in Bandera." MacNeil just said that he didn't want the headline to read "Kinky Friedman Sees Man Killed."

As I walked the cobbled streets, visited pubs and restaurants, played songs, and did interviews with the BBC, the subject of President Bush and Iraq popped up often, sometimes acrimoniously. I found myself defending my president, my country, and my cowboy hat. Soon I was going on the preemptive attack myself, calling every mild-mannered Brit who engaged me in conversation a "crumpet-chomping, Neville Chamberlain, surrender monkey." After a while, I realized the futility of this approach and merely told people that I was from a mental hospital and was going to kill them.

Bright and early the next morning, my journalist friend Ned

Temko took me on a quest for Cuban cigars, which are legal in London, if expensive. Everything is legal in London, if expensive. Phil the Tobacconist mentioned that Fidel Castro personally supplies Cuban cigars to Saddam Hussein. "I wouldn't write about that," said Ned. "George W. might nuke Fidel." As the three of us entered the walk-in humidor, Ned revealed that he'd once covered Iraq for the *Christian Science Monitor* in the late seventies. "Saddam's a thug with an excellent tailor," Ned said.

"I know his tailor," Phil said. "He's right down the street, in Savile Row."

Meeting Saddam's tailor is almost as special as meeting Gandhi's barber, but I felt I had to try. Ned, my Virgil of Savile Row, led us down the winding streets to a discreet-looking row of shops where tweeds were being measured for dukes and dictators behind closed shutters. Maybe it was the cowboy hat and high rodeo drag that prevented entry, or maybe it was simply the lack of an appointment, but at the designated address, no one came to the door. My outfit did get an enthusiastic response, however, from a group of city workers repairing the street nearby. They stopped what they were doing and sang cheerfully together, "I'm a rhinestone cowboy!"

"Since we didn't see Saddam's tailor," Ned said, "why don't we try to meet Tony Blair?"

"Jesus," I said.

"That's what the Yanks may think," said Ned. "Over here, they're about to crucify him."

Twenty minutes later, we were standing next to a Wimbledon-style grass tennis court hidden in the heart of London. "We may be in luck," said Ned. "There's Mike Levy." Levy,

Ned explained, was a former record producer who'd given the world early-seventies glam rocker Alvin Stardust. "What's he done for us lately?" I wanted to know.

"He's Tony Blair's tennis partner," he said.

Levy was in a hurry, and it didn't seem likely that Blair had played tennis that morning. Still, ever the innocent American, I stepped forward as Levy was climbing into his roadster.

"Anything you'd like to say about Tony Blair?" I asked.

"Yes," Levy said. "He needs to work on his backhand."

On my last night in London, I walked through the fog until I came to the most famous address in the world, 221B Baker Street. On the door was a small bronze plaque that read "Visitors for Mr. Sherlock Holmes or Doctor Watson please ring the bell." I rang the bell, walked up one flight of seventeen steps, and suddenly I was standing in Sherlock Holmes's living room. There was a cheery fire in the fireplace. Holmes's violin stood poignantly nearby, along with the old Persian slipper where he kept his Turkish tobacco. And in the room were Japanese, Russians, Africans, people from seemingly every nation on earth, all bound together by a common, passionate belief that Sherlock Holmes was real. It was, I thought, a perfect United Nations.

The next morning I was waiting in line at the airport to board a plane back to the States. Behind me was a proper British couple with a shy little girl clutching her teddy bear and staring intently at my hat. "Ever seen a real cowboy before?" I asked.

"No," she said. "But I've seen a cow."

CLIFF HANGER

On the night of December 17, 1998, I clung precariously to life, sanity, and a sheer cliff-side overlooking an angry sea. My only companions were lizards, iguanas, and the pale light of the Mexican moon shining like a white, luminous buttock in the mariachi sky. I'd been staying just outside Cabo San Lucas at the mansion of my friend John McCall, had taken a solitary pre-dinner power walk on the beach, and had been swept out into the ocean by a freak wave. The undertow, which killed a person that same night, swept me hundreds of yards away from the beach and deposited me at the base of a steep cliff. I tried to scramble up, but I found myself trapped between the tide and the darkness. As the water pounded ever higher along the black, crumbling landscape, intimations of mortality flooded my fevered brain. Like Arafat after his plane crash in the desert, I vowed to be a different kind of person if I survived. I thought of my mother and my cat, both of whom had gone to Jesus. I realized that I might now be seeing them sooner rather than later.

I also thought of what a bothersome housepest I'd turned out to be for my generous host, John McCall. McCall, who is also known as the Shampoo King from Dripping Springs, could afford to be generous. He runs the beauty supply company Armstrong McCall and, as he once told me, is a "centimillionaire." For those of us who can't count that high, it means McCall is worth a hundred million dollars. Even with inflation, that's not too bad. "Shampoo," says McCall, "makes people feel good about themselves."

As I held on desperately to the cliff, I took some comfort in knowing that McCall had more money than God. There was no way, I figured, he would allow his favorite Jewboy to die an untimely death without launching a land, air, and sea search. As I shivered in the darkness, I listened for helicopters that never came and resolved that if McCall wasn't thinking of me, I would think of him, thereby goosing him into action.

I thought of how McCall had been through hell a couple of times and come out laughing at the devil. In 1990 he himself had almost gone belly-up. Medical experts diagnosed him with deadly lymphoma and pointed the bone at him, giving him only weeks to live. Yet incredibly, McCall had a dream aboard an airplane in which the cancer turned to water and disappeared. When he went in for his next examination, the cancer was, in fact, gone. The doctors had never seen anything like it, but of course, that's what they usually say. Either that or you'll never walk again. McCall did, indeed, beat the first cancer, and when it returned years later, he beat it again. In the interval, just to keep in practice, he survived a plane crash in Alaska.

Now, as I clung to the cliff, soaking wet and shivering in the predawn moonscape, I hoped some of McCall's vaunted luck would rub off on me. What I didn't know that fateful night was that McCall was not really looking for me at all. It wasn't until later that morning, when he discovered my passport, cash, and cigars still in my luggage, that he swung into action. By this time I was dehydrated, delirious, and waving frantically to every fishing vessel I could see, many of whom waved back cheerfully or held up their catch of the day. Because I was trapped, ironically, on a private beach beneath luxury homes, they had no idea that the date on my carton was rapidly expiring. But McCall knew how to launch a major campaign. Soon the FBI, CIA, and DEA were involved, Don Imus's private jet was standing ready in New York, PI Steve Rambam had been consulted, and a large blowup of my passport photo, which strongly resembled a Latin American drug kingpin, could be seen on flyers on every telephone pole, hotel, hospital, morgue, and whorehouse in the greater Cabo area.

I, of course, knew none of this. I just kept concentrating on McCall, hoping I was getting through. I visualized a world traveler with a large wad of cash he calls "whip-out." I pictured a mysterious magnate who happily worked as a roadie selling T-shirts on my recent concert tour of Europe. A man

CALLAHAN

"Basically what I hear you saying, Mr. Smith, is help."

who makes huge donations to worthy causes almost always under the name Anonymous. A man who invites the Dallas Cowboys cheerleaders to his birthday parties, which he often doesn't attend himself. A man with a gazillion-dollar home outside Austin that is known as the Taj McCall. Yet money, I reflected, never seems to make people happy. As McCall himself once told me, "Happiness is a moving target."

Late in the afternoon, my hopes were fading. If I survived, I vowed, they could give me a goat's head and I'd dance all night. Once again I began stumbling upward, lost in the rocky landscape, trying to find a way to the top of my upscale death trap. Suddenly, while climbing a steep ledge, I was miraculously plucked from my precipice by an intrepid band of Mexicans who were rappelling downward. They had been working on Sly Stallone's house, and McCall had commandeered them.

Fortunately, they knew exactly where to look: The same thing had happened to another person just weeks earlier. Sly was not home at the time, but McCall was waiting at the top with a warm hug and cold cerveza. To paraphrase my father, it felt almost good to be alive.

That night, after *ocho* tequilas, I asked McCall what took him so long. He explained that he didn't take my disappearance seriously at first. McCall remembered a conversation the two of us had had several years earlier when we toured the Australian Outback. We had discussed how easy it would be for a person to disappear if he wanted to. McCall, in other words, was convinced that my absence was staged, quite possibly as some kind of publicity stunt. I'd never been averse to a little publicity, of course. I just didn't want to die from exposure.

Some days later, without pulling any punches, McCall finally revealed to me the thing that might have been the toughest blow of all. "The real tragedy," he said, "is that you were fifteen minutes away from making CNN."

ROBERT LOUIS STEVENSON IN SAMOA

Robert Louis Stevenson's dark, gypsy eyes always reminded me of Anne Frank's or Elvis's or those of some other hauntingly familiar death-bound passenger of life. They seem to burn with a fever, like embers from that borrowed campfire that provided heat and light to Stevenson's work and to his life. A piece of spiritual trivia, which some may find poignant and some may find stultifyingly dull, is that RLS, during the last five years of his life, possessed the only working fireplace in Samoa. Still, it was not enough to warm his shivering Scottish soul.

What, you might ask, does a cowboy know about Robert Louis Stevenson? What could someone from Texas, where we have wide-open spaces between our ears, possibly hope to accomplish by hectoring the people of Scotland regarding their worst legal scholar and greatest literary lighthouse keeper? We'll see.

In the meantime, we can all agree that heroes are for export. In America, for instance, we often have to remind ourselves that JFK is not just an airport, RFK is not just a football stadium, and Martin Luther King is not just a street running through the town. RLS is another set of initials representing a man who aspired to inspire before he expired and, by any account, succeeded beyond his wildest dreams. But just like many New Yorkers hardly notice the Statue of Liberty, Stevenson, perhaps understandably, may be old news to some of you. Yet RLS and the Statue of Liberty have this in common: They've both managed to shine their lights for a long time now, and mankind has managed to follow these beacons through many dark and stormy nights of human history. When we get to the destination, of course, we usually discover that it's only Joan of Arc with her hair on fire.

Writing fiction, I've always believed, is the very best way of sailing dangerously close to the truth without sinking the ship. Stevenson did this as well as anybody when he was alive and, incredibly, in this age of attention deficit disorder, still appears to be going strong. His spirit seems to transcend the time he never had and the geography he never got enough of. I have followed his footsteps, like a spiritual stalker in the sands of the South Seas, and everywhere I went it was almost impossible to believe that more than a century has passed since he was bugled to Jesus.

One of the things that makes Stevenson so enduring and appealing is that before he hit the literary big time, he was, for many colorful, quixotic, heartbreaking, bohemian years, a jet-set gypsy. Today we probably would have thought of him as a homeless person with a sparkle in his eye. Guesthouses he was summarily thrown out of now bear his name. There is a rustic area in Northern California where he wandered in deep despair and aching loneliness on a donkey, to paraphrase Leonard Cohen, like some Joseph looking for a manger. He fell off the donkey into a canyon bed and, in a weakened state of a fragile life, no doubt would have perished forgotten if he hadn't been discovered by two teenage boys. The rustic area is now known as the Robert Louis Stevenson National Forest.

In 1889, Stevenson, aboard the ninety-four-foot schooner the *Casco,* departed San Francisco, sailed the South Seas, and, seven months later, arrived safely at the harbor in Honolulu. He was beginning the mortal coda of his life. He was thirty-nine years old. He had five years left to live and die in the paradise of his choosing.

The beautiful thing about inspiration is that it travels so well. Stevenson's trip to Samoa had been deeply influenced by his reading of Herman Melville, whom Stevenson, like almost everybody else, assumed was dead. Melville wasn't dead, however, he was just not currently working on a project. He was living out his last days as customs inspector #75 in New York. *Moby Dick* had already been out for almost forty years and could still only be found in the whaling sections of bookstores. "The important books," Melville had said, "are the books that fail." When he died in 1891, the *New York Times* misspelled his name in its obituary. By then, of course, Stevenson was safely ensconced in Samoa.

In the time he had left, Stevenson's family grew, from his wife, Fanny, her son, Lloyd, and his mother, Margaret, to spiritually encompass almost the entire Samoan people. He had a romantic, some might say misguided, view of the Polynesian race in general. He believed they had the brains, beauty, and spirit of the ancient Greeks, and that if the world would leave them alone, they would blossom and flourish, becoming the centerpiece on the table of modern civilization. Needless to say, this was not a view shared by the Americans, the British, or the Germans, all of whom had designs on Samoa.

Thus it was that Stevenson found himself supporting a local chieftain named Mataafa, a rebel Robin Hood who stood squarely in the way of the powers that be. By this time RLS was already a beloved cultural icon in Samoa. In the mountain of almost a million words he piled up over his lifetime was the Samoan translation of his South Seas story "The Bottle Imp." It was the first fiction any of the Samoans had ever read in their own language, and many of them, perhaps quite correctly, concluded that fiction might just be another way of telling the truth. Many Samoans, indeed, came to believe that the real bottle imp resided in the big safe in the big house on Stevenson's plantation, Vailima.

Stevenson was soon accorded the accolade *Tusitala*, or The Storyteller, a title of great spiritual importance in Samoan culture. There was probably a bit of Lord Jim and a bit of Don

Quixote in Stevenson's relationship with the native islanders, not to mention a scrap of Sergeant Pepper's Lonely and a shard of Gullible's Travels. But this was as it should be, for Stevenson, like the Samoans, was a childlike, romantic, exuberant spirit, and he fit into paradise with the same awkward grace that he fit into the limbo of the white man's world.

RLS might have been the only white man on the planet who believed that Mataafa could be king of the Samoans and that it was important for this to come to pass. It was in this spirit that Stevenson interceded when Mataafa and his followers were captured and imprisoned, gaining the freedom of most of the political prisoners. In gratitude to Tusitala, these Samoans, who by nature instinctively despised manual labor, built a road from Apia, the capital, to Vailima. They named it "The Road of the Loving Hearts" and it still stands today as a monument to Stevenson's humanity.

You can drive this road, as I did some years ago, all the way to Vailima, which is now a beautiful museum and library. You can also climb the nearby Mount Vaea, which I did as well, stand amidst the windy majesty of the glittering Pacific, and commune with the lingering presence of RLS. On the side of his tomb, two verses are inscribed from his poem "Requiem":

> Under the wide and starry sky
> Dig the grave and let me lie
> For glad did I live and glad did I die
> And I laid me down with a will.

And these be the words you 'grave for me
Here he lies where he longed to be
Home is the sailor, home from the sea
And the hunter, home from the hill.

There is some special something about the way in which Stevenson passionately interwove his evanescent life with his incredible art that has caused the ensuing embroidery to seem to last forever. Like van Gogh, like Hank Williams, the work defines, sustains, and sometimes destroys its creator. Robert Louis Stevenson's magic is that he gives it to you.

Before he ever got to Samoa, while still in Hawaii, RLS befriended the young Princess Kaiulani and read to her often under their special banyan tree. Kaiulani, another death-bound passenger of life, was the last princess of Hawaii, soon to lose her kingdom, her poetic friend, and her own life at the age of twenty-three as the people of Hawaii and her royal peacocks all cried together. The banyan tree was eventually cut down by the rough hand of progress, but someone was wise enough to save a green branch, which now has grown into a beautiful tree gracing the playground of Princess Kaiulani Elementary School in Honolulu. Beneath the tree is a bronze plaque that bears a verse from a poem Stevenson wrote for her before she left for schooling in Britain.

Forth from her land to mine she goes,
The island maid, the island rose,
Light of heart and bright of face:

The daughter of a double race.
Her islands here, in Southern sun,
Shall mourn their Kaiulani gone,
And I, in her dear banyan shade,
Look vainly for my little maid.

Stevenson also visited the island of Molokai, shortly after the death of the great holy man Father Damien, whom he very much admired. While there he taught croquet to the leprosy patients at the girls' school. The ephemeral act of teaching croquet to young leprosy patients speaks like a living page torn from Stevenson's own short, afflicted life. As he left for the barge, the young students crowded along the fence to say goodbye. Had he not left then, Stevenson wrote, he would never have been able to.

And in Samoa to this day there is a traditional greeting sometimes given to ship captains and passengers who arrive by sea. Part of the native greeting is a question that translates into English in roughly the following manner: "Is Mr. Robert Louis Stevenson aboard your ship?" There is no easy answer to this metaphysical question. I would like to think, however, that the answer is "Yes, and he always will be."

WATCH WHAT
YOU SING

I was having a cup of coffee one morning in the hostility suite of the mental hospital when my editor called and suggested I write about the Dixie Chicks. I told him that by the time I finished writing about them, people would be asking, "The Dixie *who*?"

"No," he said. "They'll be a topic of heated debate for some time. Just ask your fellow residents."

So I did. I asked a 275-pound, six-foot-tall black man who was under the impression that he was Napoleon. "Sure," he said. "I loved the Dixie Chicks. They were cute and little and purple. They wiggled through a fence in Houston fifty years ago and were eaten by two dachshunds."

"No," I told him. "Those were the Easter chicks."

So I took the elevator up to my padded room in the van Gogh wing, where I live with my pet typewriter. But I wasn't sure what to type. I didn't know a hell of a lot about the Dixie Chicks, but I did know their agent, Dr. Kevorkian. I called him on a secure line.

"Hey, Doc," I said, "how are things goin' with the Chicks?"

"Great!" he said. "Not only are they riding high on the charts here in the States, but they're also moving into heavy rotation on the new country station in Tikrit."

"That's wonderful!" I said. "How's the tour going?"

"Fantastic!" he said. "We're selling out every date. And this summer we've been invited to open for Jerry Lewis on a tour of France."

"How do you explain the rather odd phenomenon," I asked, "of the Chicks going up on the pop charts at the same time they were going down on the country charts?"

"What," he asked, "do those country hicks know about music?"

By the time I hung up with the good doctor, I had an even more confused image of who the Chicks were. Was it healthy for me to be listening to their music? Were they trying to poison my values? Were they trying to poison my soup? I had to know the answer to that last one right away, because the sign in the lobby read TODAY IS TUESDAY. THE NEXT MEAL IS LUNCH.

At lunch I talked to a woman who was sitting at my table, and I asked her what she thought of the Chicks. "I'm going to an ophthalmologists' convention in Las Vegas," she said.

I asked, "Do you think they really should've told a European audience that they were ashamed President Bush came from Texas?"

The woman, in a far deeper, far more bitter voice, answered, "Mother Mary, full of grace, help me find a parking place."

"One more question, if you don't mind," I said. "Do you think the issue of freedom of speech comes into play here? I mean, surely the Dixie Chicks can say what they like onstage or off, but should they be held accountable for their behavior? Or, conversely, do you think bad behavior should be rewarded by a measurable increase of success in the marketplace?"

"I've eaten an appropriate amount for my figure!" the woman screamed in a frightening falsetto. She was becoming increasingly agitated. As an orderly took her away, I wondered whether she hated the Dixie Chicks or just didn't want Jell-O for dessert.

I went back to my room after lunch in something of a petulant snit myself. I was starting to get a rather negative impression of the Chicks. No one in the hospital seemed to have heard of them. Was it possible that they didn't really exist at all? Could it be they were merely a figment of the American imagination? An abstract notion to which we all subscribed? A supreme being in whom we all believed? Were the Dixie Chicks God? "Blasphemous!" I thought. "Impossible!" Yet nobody seemed to know who or what they really were or stood for. And, I was forced to admit, they had pretty much risen from the dead. I bowed my head to pray.

When I looked up, the room was bathed in a strange incandescent, celestial light. Either I was in heaven or inside an old-fashioned jukebox. The Dixie Chicks were on my television set, singing to me in perfect harmony. The lyrics, as best as I can remember, went something like this:

> We're sorry if we hurt the president's feelers
> But he wasn't nice like that Garrison Keillors
> We're not ashamed that we said what we meant
> Now tell us why you're a wig-city resident.

"That's what I want to know," I said. "The shrink claimed he put me in here because I believe I'm George Bush's rabbi. But I *am* George Bush's rabbi! I told that shrink, 'For God's sake, Hoss! You can't put George Bush's rabbi in a mental hospital! I'm ashamed that you come from New Jersey.'"

"We know how you feel," said the Dixie Chicks, who were now no longer on my television screen but standing in the padded room with me. "We've gone through something like that ourselves. You didn't do anything wrong. You were just misunderstood."

"Damn right!" I said. "I don't belong in here."

"Of course you don't," said the Dixie Chicks. "After all, you're George Bush's rabbi, and he needs all the guidance he can get. Now, before we leave for our sold-out national tour, how'd you like it if we sang for you again?"

"Make it brief," I said. "The Pope's calling at two o'clock."

And then they sang, and their voices were so beautiful and innocent that I could imagine what they must have been like when they were just three little girls growing up in the country, never dreaming that one day they'd be pestering the president and posing nude on the cover of a magazine. But I'll always remember the verse they sang to me. I think it's from some old gospel song:

Lord, we have sinned
But who among us
Ever really dances
With the one who brung us?

PART V

ADVICE ON COMING HOME

CALLAHAN

"I'd like to thank all who made it possible for me
to be here tonight."

A LITTLE NIGHT MUSIC

L eaving the frenetic ant farm that is now Austin, in this year of our Lord 2001, you can set your ears back as you head west on U.S. 290. Pretty soon you're in the rolling Hill Country, and you realize why they say Texas is a state of mind. It's nighttime, and the cowboy stars are shining; it could be any time and any highway. So you lose track of time and let it flow back; suddenly you're in the fifties. The fifties in Texas may not have been the Paris of the twenties, but how many different kinds of sauces can you put on a chicken-fried steak?

You're blowing through Dripping Springs, and the hills are dark shadows; the highway's just a ribbon in the hair of a girl you used to know. Maybe Hank Williams is on the radio. Actually, you're probably a little late for Hank since he died on

January 1, 1953, en route to a show in Canton, Ohio. You can't blame him, really. Some people will do anything to avoid a gig in Canton.

Now Charlie Walker's on the radio with his hit song, "Pick Me Up on Your Way Down." Charlie now plays on the Grand Ole Opry. He says he used to own a club in San Antonio called the Old Barn, and that he booked Hank there for one of his last shows in Texas. It was also Hank's last birthday, September 17, 1952. Hank had the number-one song in the country, "Jambalaya." Charlie says he paid him five hundred bucks—a lot of money in 1952. Of course, it's nothing today. The value of the dollar and almost everything else has tanked pretty severely since then. Even the stars shone brighter in the fifties. Maybe it's just when you're young they appear brighter—like objects in the mirror. You know you've grown up when you realize how far you are away from the stars.

Now you're flying past Johnson City, past the little town of Luckenbach, Texas, which would someday be a famous song. Now you're getting deeper into the Hill Country and deeper into the fifties. Man has not yet landed on the moon, but he's discovered the Moon Pie. Kennedy hasn't been shot, so nobody has to remember where they were.

The car moves like a patient brushstroke through the sepia night, through the towns of Fredericksburg and then Kerrville, sleepy and sprinkled with lights. The shadows of the hills are bigger and darker, and the same stars above you swear that she loves you, that she is your pretty fraulein. And hundreds of miles away to the west, across the aching emptiness, the land is flat again, and a young Buddy Holly is setting out to prove that the world isn't square.

As you drive, he's probably sitting in his car staying up half the night listening to a rhythm-and-blues program out of Shreveport. It is 1951 in Lubbock, Texas, and it is the miles and miles of aching emptiness all around him, that spiritual elbow-room, that creates the climate for something new to strike the world like a Texas blue norther. Bob Wills and Elvis came through Lubbock in 1955, and not long after that Buddy was on his way past time and geography to that borrowed campfire that warms the world.

There were not going to be any happy endings. Hank would die in a Cadillac. Buddy would die in a plane. Elvis would die on a toilet. Bob Wills would die broke. Today, of course, we realize that none of them will ever die. But back in the fifties they were as alive as you and me; Cadillacs were getting longer, tail fins were getting higher; and dreams were getting as close as they ever do to coming true.

GOD'S OWN COWBOYS

L ast weekend, Barry Goldwater, Chuck Conners ("The Rifleman") and James Drury ("The Virginian") were inducted into the National Cowboy Hall of Fame in Oklahoma City. Without taking away from this trio's status as fine Americans, one must wonder if the inductors might not have reached a bit spiritually in calling them cowboys.

Far be it for me to suggest that they were not cowboys, for cowboys come in all colors and denominations. My only contention is that the final arbiters of what is a cowboy should be God and small children, and I'm not certain they would have chosen this particular trinity. But let us explore this wandering trail together.

Though Spanish-speaking peoples, it should be noted, are

quite often mean to bulls, they did give us the first rodeos in Mexico, in the 1700s. In fact, much of what was to become the cowboy derived from the Spanish *vaquero*. The first rodeos as we know them in the United States came about a century later and often featured black cowboys. The Cowboy Hall of Fame tells me that its "minority category" (in which all cowboys actually belong) consists of "two Mexicans, two black cowboys, one Native American, and no cowboys recognized as Jewish."

Tom Mix, who is a member, was said to be half Jewish, and Wyatt Earp was married to a Jewish dancehall girl—but close only counts in horseshoes. Being Jewish and having lived in the Texas Hill Country most of my life, the only thing I've seen that Jews and cowboys seem to have in common is that both wear their hats indoors and attach a certain amount of importance to it.

One of the few real cowboys I know is a man named Earl Buckelew, who has lived all of his life in the heart of the Hill Country near Medina, Texas. For more than seventy-six years, Earl has lived on the land, ridden the range, and loved and understood horses. And, what is even rarer, he loves and understands himself. These days, Earl lives in a trailer and watches *Wheel of Fortune*. He was not inducted into the Cowboy Hall of Fame, but then, Nellie Fox hasn't made it into the Baseball Hall of Fame yet either.

The notion of the cowboy has always been one of America's most precious gifts to the children of the world. Indeed, the early cowboys, whether they drove down the Chisholm Trail or Sunset Boulevard, reached higher into the firmament than they might have known. When Anne Frank's secret annex was revisited after World War II, pictures of American cowboy stars were still fluttering from the walls where she had left them.

True cowboys must be able to ride beyond time and geography. They must leave us a dream to grow by, a haunting echo of a song, a fine dust that is visible for generations against even a black and white sunset. Today many children of the dust dream of becoming cowboys.

God bless 'em. Most of them probably won't achieve that difficult, poetical, impractical, but not impossible dream. Some of them, however, might just make it. I sure hope they do because I believe that within the soul of every cowboy shines a spirit that might just save us from ourselves.

SHOSHONE THE MAGIC PONY

A happy childhood, I've always believed, is the worst possible preparation for life. Life is so different from childhood, it seems. The magic tricks have all been explained to us. The sparkle, we now realize, is all passive smoke and rearview mirrors. Maybe things were always this way, but I don't really think so. I think there was a time.

In 1953, when I was about seven years old, my parents took me to see Shoshone the Magic Pony. That was also the year that Tom and Min Friedman bought Echo Hill Ranch and turned it into a children's camp, providing thousands of boys and girls with many happy, carefree summers of fun. But although 1953 might've been a good year for the Friedmans and a good year for wine, it'd been a bad year for almost everybody and everything else. Hank Williams, along with Julius and Ethel Rosenberg, had checked out of the mortal motel that year, quite possibly unaware that the other party had been there to begin with. Hank fried his brains and heart and other internal organs for our sins, using eleven different kinds of herbs and spices. Julius and Ethel, charged with spying for Russia, many thought falsely, were fried by our government and died declaring their innocence and their love for each other. Hank's songs declared his innocence and his love, inexplicably, for people. It is doubtful whether Hank and the Rosenbergs had anything in common at all, except that a small boy in Texas had cried when each of them died.

The boy had also cried the year before when Adlai Stevenson had lost the potato-sack hop at the company picnic to good ol' Ike, the Garth Brooks of all presidents, who turned out to be the most significant leader we'd had since Millard Fillmore and remained as popular as the bottle of ketchup on the kitchen table of America, even if Lenny Bruce and Judy Garland, who were destined to both die on toilets, like Elvis, remained in their rooms for the entire two terms of his presidency.

The kid had seemed to cry a bit back then, but fortunately, human tragedies of this sort never cut into his happy childhood. When he grew up, he continued to cry at times, though the tears were no longer visible in or to the naked eye, for he never let human tragedies of this sort cut into his cocktail hour. But during his childhood, it is very likely that his parents noticed the tears. That may have been the reason they took him to see Shoshone the Magic Pony.

These days, as we peer cautiously out across the grey listless afternoon that is adulthood, we seek and we find fewer and fewer surprises in life. What dreams we have are veiled in memory, etched in regret. Our minds go back to yesterday street and the summertime of our choosing. Maybe it's 1953. Maybe it's a little rodeo arena near Bandera, Texas, where the loud-speaker had just announced Shoshone the Magic Pony. My father and mother, Tom and Min, were sitting on the splintery bleachers next to me and my little brother Roger. And suddenly, all our eyes were on the center of the arena.

Shoshone came out prancing, led by an old cowboy with a big white beard. He took the reins and bridle off Shoshone and the horse bowed several times to the audience. Shoshone had a beautiful saddle and a large saddle blanket that seemed to glitter with sequins of red, white, and blue. Then the old cowboy stood back and the music began. It was "The Tennessee Waltz." And Shoshone the Magic Pony started to dance.

It was apparent from the outset, even to us children in the crowd, that there were two men inside the body of Shoshone. You could tell by the clever, intricate soft-shoe routine she was performing, by the fact that she often appeared to be moving hilariously in two directions at once, and by the funny and very unponylike way she now and again humped and arched her back to the music. I was laughing so hard I forgot for the moment about Hank Williams, Adlai Stevenson, the Rosenbergs, and myself. Whoever was inside there was so good, I even forgot that they were inside there.

Then "The Tennessee Waltz" was over.

Shoshone bowed a deep, theatrical bow. Everybody laughed and clapped and cheered. The old cowboy took off his hat. Then he took off his beard. Then he took off the old cowboy mask he was wearing and we saw to our amazement that the old-timer was in reality a very pretty young girl.

She took off Shoshone's saddle. Then she took off her saddle blanket. And there, to my total astonishment, stood only Shoshone the Magic Pony.

Shoshone was a real horse.

In the years that followed, as I grew up or simply got older, Shoshone served me well as a reminder of the duplicitous nature of man. Nothing is what it appears to be, I thought. But there are times when with awkward grace the odd comfort of this crazy world comes inexplicably close to my crazy heart. At times like these, I see Shoshone as a shining symbol of the galloping faith that some horses and some people will always remain exactly who they are.

THE HUMMINGBIRD
MAN

A wise old man named Slim, who wore a paper Rainbow bread cap, drank warm Jax beer in infinite quantities, listened faithfully to the hapless Houston Astros on the radio, and washed dishes at our family's ranch, once told me something I've never forgotten. He said, "You're born alone and you die alone, so you might as well get used to it." It didn't mean much to me then, but over the years I've come to believe that old Slim might have been on to something.

I live alone now in the lodge, where my late parents once lived, and I'm getting used to it. Being a member of the Orphan Club is not so bad. Sooner or later, fate will pluck us all up by our pretty necks. If you have a family of your own, maybe you won't feel it quite as much. Or maybe you will. I'm married to the wind, and my children are my animals and the books I've written, and I love them all. I don't play favorites. But I miss my mom and dad. In the past fifty years, thousands of kids have known Uncle Tom and Aunt Min. They bought our ranch outside Medina in 1953, named it Echo Hill, and made it into a camp for boys and girls. Echo Hill will be open again this summer, and though the kids will ride horses, swim in the river, and explore the hills, they will not get to meet Uncle Tom and Aunt Min.

My mother died in May 1985, just a few weeks before camp started, and my father died in August 2002, just a few weeks after camp was over. I can still see my mother at her desk, going over her cluttered clipboard with all the camp rosters and menus. I can see her at the Navajo campfire, at the big hoedown, at the friendship circle under the stars. I can see my dad wearing a pith helmet and waving to the kids in the charter buses. I can see him raising the flag in the morning, slicing the watermelon at picnic suppers, sitting in a lawn chair out in front of the lodge, talking patiently to a kid having problems with his bunkmates. If you saw him sitting quietly there, you'd think he was talking to one of his old friends. Many of those kids became just that.

I don't know how many baby fawns ago it was, how many stray dogs and cats ago, or how many homesick kids ago, but fifty years is a long time in camp years. Yet time, as they say, is the money of love. And Tom and Min put a lot of all those things into Echo Hill. Most of their adult lives were given over to children, daddy longlegs, arrowheads, songs, and stars. They lived in a little green valley surrounded by gentle hills, where the sky was as blue as the river, the river ran pure, the waterfalls sparkled clear in the summer sun, and the campfire embers never really seemed to die. I was just a kid, but looking back, that's the way I remember it.

What I remember most of all are the hummingbirds. It might have been 1953 when my mother hung out the first hummingbird feeder on the front porch of the lodge. The grown-up, outside world liked Ike that year and loved Lucy, and Hank Williams died, as did Ethel and Julius Rosenberg. I believe now that I might have been vaguely aware of these things occurring even back then, but it was those tiny, wondrous rainbows of flying color that really caught my eye. And those first few brave hummingbirds had come thousands of miles, all the way from Mexico and Central America, just to be with us at Echo Hill. Every year the hummers would make this long migration, arriving almost precisely on March 15, the Ides of March. They would leave late in the summer, their departure usually depending upon how much fun they had had at camp.

For those first few years, in the early fifties, the hummingbird population, as well as the number of campers, was fairly sparse, but as the green summers flashed by, more and more kids and hummingbirds came to Echo Hill. The hummingbirds nested every year in the same juniper tree next to the lodge. Decades later, after my mother's death, the tree began to die as well. Yet even when there were only a few green branches left, the hummers continued to make that tree their summer home. Some of the staff thought the tree was an eyesore and more than once offered to cut it down, but Tom wouldn't hear of it. I think he regarded the hummingbirds as little pieces of my mother's soul.

My father and I more or less took over the hummingbird program together in 1985. As time went by, we grew into the job. It was amazing how creatures so tiny could have such a profound influence on your peace of mind and the way you looked at the world. My father, of course, did many other things besides feeding the hummingbirds. I, unfortunately, did not. That was how I gradually came to be known as the Hummingbird Man of Echo Hill.

Tom and I disagreed, sometimes almost violently, about the feeding methods for these fragile little creatures. He measured exactly four scoops of sugar and two drops of red food coloring into the water for each feeder. I eyeballed the whole process, using much more sugar and blending many weird colors into the mix. Whatever our disagreements over methodology, the hummer population grew. This past summer, it registered more than a hundred birds at "happy hour." Tom confided to me that once, long ago, he mixed a little gin in with the hummers' formula and they seemed to have a particularly lively happy hour. Min was not happy about it, however, and firmly put a stop to this practice.

Now, on bright, cold mornings, I stand in front of the old lodge, squinting into the brittle Hill Country sunlight, hoping, I suppose, for an impossible glimpse of a hummingbird or of my mother or my father. They've all migrated far away, and the conventional wisdom is that only the hummingbirds are ever coming back. Yet I still see my mother hanging up that first feeder. The juniper tree blew down in a storm two winters ago, but the hummers have found other places to nest. One of them is in my heart.

And I still see my dad sitting under the dead juniper tree, only the tree doesn't seem dead, and neither does he. It takes a big man to sit there with a little hummingbird book, taking the time to talk to a group of small boys. He is telling them that there are more than three hundred species of hummingbirds. They are the smallest of all birds, he says, and also the fastest. They're also, he tells the kids, the only birds who can fly backwards. The little boys seem very excited about the notion of flying backwards. They'd like to try that themselves, they say. So would I.

HOW TO HANDLE A NONSTOP TALKER IN A POST-9/11 WORLD

No person is immune to the Nonstop Talker. They lurk everywhere there is an audience and like a spider, they wait patiently for their prey to approach and unwittingly become entangled in their web. Once they have you, they assault you with their blather, and the harder you struggle to get free, the more entangled you become until you are paralyzed by their words and consumed from the inside out, drained of all energy and life force. Encountering a Nonstop Talker on foot is exhausting but doable. When you've had enough, you can simply run or drive away. Getting stuck next to one on a long flight, however, is like being banished to the ninth level of Dante's Inferno and will require extensive counseling for post-tedium stress disorder, if you survive the catastrophe.

Studies on lab rats have shown that there is no sure way to "talk-block" the Nonstop Talker but there are some techniques I have used that had limited success; I can't guarantee these will work for you but doing them may at least make you feel like you are being proactive rather than just a passive victim. That alone gives your subsequent trauma counseling a much greater chance of succeeding.

The suggestions I outline below can be done in any order. It's best to practice the techniques at home in front of a mirror before using them in a real situation so they will be second nature when you need them.

Now, imagine you've boarded an airplane, you've strapped yourself in, and you're settling back to enjoy the oxygen-mask tutorial performed by a peppy flight attendant named "Colt." Suddenly you hear a distant whining sound, like a mosquito in your ear, and to your horror you realize you are seated next to a Nonstop Talker! The first thing to do is *remain calm*. Take a deep breath and do a body check. Make sure you have not reactively assumed the fetal position because if you want to survive this encounter, you have to allow the blood to flow to all your extremities lest you develop deep vein thrombosis, a deadly blood clot that starts in your calf and travels to your lungs and kills you.

By the time the plane clears the runway and attains liftoff, Nonstop Talker will have already tangented about six times without closing anything he says (since this is a worst-case scenario, I use the Tangenter, who is the worst kind of Nonstop Talker; listening to one talk is like reading a page full of left parentheses without any closing parentheses). You have a couple of choices now. You can sit still and allow his words to flow over you like the Grim Reaper over a grave or you can go ahead and start trying some of my suggestions as listed below. Don't wait too long to act because if you let Nonstop Talker blather on unrestrained, you could spontaneously combust, and fires are illegal on commercial airlines. The only thing worse than flying with a Nonstop Talker is being incarcerated in a federal prison with one doing life without parole for breaching air safety regulations.

Nonstop Talker will be saying something like this (and this is just an example. No one really hears what they say. I just want to get you into the moment): "Don't you hate it when your story doesn't hold up in court and you have to come up with an alibi that doesn't put you anywhere near that all-boy's private school on the day in question? Has that ever happened to you? Well, I was walking down this dead-end street and decided to get a cream cheese bagel . . ."

At this point you can begin your response. Again, these suggestions can be done in any order, and feel free to improvise. Every Nonstop Talker is different, so use what you think will be most effective against them in your situation.

Good luck and Godspeed.

RESPONSES TO A NONSTOP TALKER

Put on your headphones. You don't actually have to have an mp3 or CD player; you can just tuck the unplugged end into your empty pocket. It really helps the visuals if you use the white I-pod earphones because they will stand out against any kind of travel wardrobe.

Pretend that you're listening to gangsta rap music. Most people who travel in the first-class section fear and loathe rap. Sing along with your imaginary Grandmasta Houseshoes collection. Throw gang signs and breakdance in your seat.

Exhibit symptoms of Tourette's Syndrome. Emphasize the yelping and swearing part.

Act like you've fallen asleep. Just close your eyes and let your chin drop to your chest. You could add a snore or two for variety. Drooling a little is also a nice touch.

Frantically rummage around for the air-sickness bag. Make loud retching sounds into it. Wonder aloud if a person can be infected with SARS twice in a lifetime.

"Your order will be ready when I yell, 'Mother-fucker.'"

Straddle the armrest between your seats and pretend that you're a rodeo cowboy only eight seconds from glory. Thrust one hand in the air and thrash your body around violently.

Retrieve the flotation device from under your seat and put it on. As you inflate it, explain that every flight you've ever been on has crashed into the sea and you just want to be ready this time.

When all else fails and you still have hours of flight time left, go ahead and curl up into that fetal position and cut loose that blood clot. With any luck, it will reach your lungs before your Nonstop Talker segues into the one about his anal fissures.

SOCIAL STUDIES

Who says Texas etiquette doesn't exist? From matters culinary to matters urinary, it defines who we are like nothing else.

To the 6.1 billion people on this planet who are not Texans, the very idea of Texas etiquette may seem like a contradiction. These culturally deprived souls, sometimes known as the rest of the world, go blithely through life believing implicitly in lady wrestlers, Catholic universities, and military intelligence, yet they scoff at the notion of Texas etiquette.

We Texans believe if it ain't King James, it ain't Bible. We believe in holding hands and saying grace before eating big, hairy steaks in chain restaurants. If the steak is the size of a sombrero, the meal is followed by the belching of the Lord's

Prayer, which is then followed by projectile vomiting. Extreme cases may result in what some Texans commonly refer to as "squirtin' out of both ends."

The only thing that really differentiates Texas from any other place in the world, however, is the proclivity of its people to urinate out of doors and to attach a certain amount of importance to this popular pastime. Urinating outside goes much further than merely meeting the criteria of what is socially acceptable; it is the way of our people. To walk out under the Texas stars and water your lizard is considered the most sacred inalienable right of all citizens of the Lone Star State.

Though Texans are always a relatively considerate bunch, things do seem to get a little wiggy when a certain type of woman meets another woman from the same substratum whom she hasn't seen since Kennedy was croaked in Dallas (which we don't really consider to be part of Texas). The announcement of JFK's death, by the way, was rumored to have been greeted with cheering in certain boardrooms and country clubs in the state, which, of course, was a mild lapse in Texas etiquette. So, no doubt, was killing President Kennedy.

As I was saying before I heard voices in my head, there is a traditional greeting used by women in Texas who haven't seen each other in a while. In a sort of latent lesbian mating ritual, the first one's face lights up insanely, and she shrieks, "Look at yeeew!" The other one, her countenance locked in an equally demonic rictus, responds, "Look at yeeew!!!" There is little doubt that this increasingly frenetic, insectile exchange would continue indefinitely if not for the intercession of a third party. Suddenly a big cowboy walks up, strikes a match on his wranglers—he has two Mexican wranglers who work for him—and proceeds to set the women on fire.

Now the women are dancing around like vapid versions of Joan of Arc, sparks flying from their big hair, still screaming "Look at yeeew!!!" and they would have no doubt fallen through the trap door in tandem if not for the appearance of another party. Fortunately a man nearby just happens to be urinating out of doors and saves the day by taking the thing into his own hands and extinguishing the fire with Hose Number One.

Sometimes Texas etiquette manifests itself far beyond the boundaries of the Lone Star State. When I was working in

Borneo with the Peace Corps, I decided to take a little trip to Thailand with a few other volunteers. This was the height of the Haight-Ashbury era and, of course, the Vietnam War. In a seedy little bar in Chiang Mai, these two forces came together. By forces, I mean special forces, as in Green Berets. A group of them, on R&R from Vietnam, had been drinking rather heavily at the bar. There were four of us Peace Corps kids, all skinny as Jesus, with long hair and native beads, and one of our party, Dylan Ferrero, happened, rather unfortunately, to be sporting a flower in his hair. In the air, the sense of impending doom was almost palpable. The Green Berets, like ourselves, had been culturally out where the buses don't run for possibly a little too long. They thought we were real hippies. And they were in no mood to let Saigons be bygones.

A wiry, dangerous-looking little Hawaiian guy from this gang wandered over with a glaze of hatred in his eyes that almost wilted Dylan's flower. I remember his words quite well because he chanted them with a soft, evil cadence: "Ain't you cool." A bar in Chiang Mai could be a godless, lawless place in 1967, almost as lawless and godless as a lonely road outside Jasper in 1998. But it was just at that moment that I thought I heard a familiar accent—a Texas accent. The deep, drawling tones were emanating from the largest man I'd ever seen. He was sitting with the Green Berets, watching the ongoing tension convention at the bar. With a sudden confidence that must have come from deep in the heart of Texas, I walked over to a table of cranked-up Special Forces. With my beads and Angela Davis Afro, it would have been the stupidest thing I'd ever done in my life if I hadn't been so sure that Goliath was from Texas. Texas saved me.

In a matter of moments, I had learned that the guy was from Dublin, Texas, and he knew my old college friend Lou Siegel, who was also from Dublin. The next thing anybody knew, the invisible bond of latent homosexual Texas manhood had transcended all the other human chemistry in the bar and the world. Years later I thanked Lou for being spiritually in the right place at the right time. I never saw Goliath the Green Beret again. Maybe he just got Starbucked into the twenty-first century like everybody else and is sipping a decaf latte somewhere and reading the *Wall Street Gerbil*.

I wish I could say that Texas etiquette really exists. Maybe it's like God or Santa Claus or brotherly love—something no one's ever seen but just might be there after all. Years ago my mother had a little sign on her desk at Echo Hill Ranch. It read: "Courtesy is owed. Respect is earned. Love is given." That may be as close to Texas etiquette as any of us will ever get.

GETTIN' MY GOAT

The Reverend Goat Carson was the last man ever to dance with Judy Garland. The place was the Salvation Club in New York City. The time was late November 1968. The Reverend Goat Carson, of course, was not a reverend back then. He wasn't even a Native American yet. He described the Judy Garland encounter as "dancing with a soft, little marshmallow with legs." Very soon thereafter she flew to London, last stop before booking a package tour with a chirpy group of bluebirds over the rainbow.

Unfortunately, Goat saved the last dance for me. We first met in L.A. in 1976, where Goat got his name. It was given to him a few years earlier, along with adult-size portions of smoke and mushrooms, by a medicine man named Yippee!, a

Yaqui Indian from Acapulco. Yippee! took the then twenty-one-year-old David Carson on a "vision quest" to show him that music was the power that would change the world. "You're a Native American," said Yippee!, and Goat told him truthfully that he was part Cherokee. That was good enough for Yippee!, apparently, who then led the young Goat to the Sunset Strip, where he introduced him to the members of a band called the Doors and one called Iron Butterfly, plied him with more marijuana and mushrooms, and then took him down to South Central to see the first American appearance of Hugh Masekela.

Somewhere in the middle of this vision quest, everything seemed to stop. Goat saw a light pulsating in his chest and realized that he was outside of time and body, watching himself in a movie. "I feel like I have the power to do anything," he said.

"Then go on and try," said Yippee! "Your name will be 'Goat,' and that will stand for Go on and try." With varying degrees of success, Goat has ever since.

I had drifted out to L.A. myself, trying to get a record deal peddling a quasi-legendary living room tape of the Texas Jewboys. Goat was living out of his car, parking it at night at Errol Flynn's house. We met as a result of both of us hanging out with Bob Dylan. Half the free world was hanging out with Bob Dylan at that time, of course; the other half was trying to understand his lyrics.

The first time Goat met Bob was at a semiexclusive Hollywood after-party at which Goat chose to perform upon his homemade instrument of choice, a three-stringed jawbone of an ass, his own version of Bob's popular song "Sarah," an elegant, poetical ode to his wife of many years. Few in the room knew that Bob and his wife would soon be going through divorce proceedings. This, indeed, may have been the mitigating factor for why Goat and his sacred jaw-bone did not get thrown out on his ass.

Goat's version of the song went something like this: "Sar—ah! Sar—ah! Spirit of dawn, child of the night / Sar—ah! Sar—ah! Shut up, you bitch. I'm tryin' to write."

A deadly silence filled the room. The faces of everyone appeared ashen with horror at this blasphemy. A large, impeccably dressed black man walked over to Goat and began gently but firmly removing the rather arcane instrument from the offending musician's cold, dead fingers. Then Bob himself got up and came over to Goat. Some strange sensibility struggled across his inscrutable countenance; every eye was upon Bob's face until at last, chimeralike, he smiled. "I like your song," he said.

Almost immediately the small crowd began laughing and chuckling. "That song actually was brilliant," the publicist observed. "I must have had a nail in my head."

Eventually, I lost touch with Goat. I went on the road with Bob, and Goat, I presumed, went with God. In those days, there sometimes didn't seem to be a hell of a lot of difference between the two. I did see Goat again in the early eighties, when I was performing at the Lone Star Café in New York, and he showed up dancing onstage, wearing a giant stuffed polar bear's head.

Goat would never speak when he wore the polar bear's head, but he would sing one song. That song was always "Big Balls in Cowtown."

But Goat Carson was much more than a helper monkey whoring himself for the amusement of the fickle masses. Goat was also a visionary, a veteran soul imbued with a deep, poetical nature that often manifested itself precisely when the chips were down. Witness this virtually spontaneous little poem Goat delivered to the crowd at the wake of our mutual friend Tom Baker in New York in 1982.

He just sat down on that same barstool,
He was still living for the day
He still wasn't worried and he still wasn't married.
Don't count on tomorrow, he'd say.
Between the gutter and the stars,
People are what people are.
Tom Baker was a friend of mine.

Our American lives had intertwined in L.A. and New York, and now they would shatter and split. After the death of the Bakerman, a personal fast-lane hero of mine, I returned to Texas while Goat remained in New York. We did not see each other for almost twenty-three years. I wasn't even aware that Goat had moved to New Orleans or that he'd become an ordained street preacher there for the past twelve years. It would require an act of God to bring us together again. An act of God in the form of a woman. Her name was Katrina.

* * *

Thus it was that on August 28, in the year of our Lord 2005, just approaching nut-cuttin' time in my campaign for governor, I received an urgent call from the man who was to become my personal evacuee for the next two years. Goat told me he'd called every rich Christian friend he had in California to no avail. It was mildly ironic, I thought at the time, that he'd be taken in by a Texas Jewboy who'd been running his campaign like his life, on a shoestring.

Goat showed up at our house in Austin in much worse shape than I'd expected. A complete emotional wreck, he walked in with nothing but the clothes on his back, a satchel containing various gris-gris concoctions, and a small bundle of sacred rabbit furs that were eaten by the dogs when I took Goat out for Mexican food. The next day we both watched New Orleans die on television. Goat had gotten out just in time.

I took Goat up to the ranch near Kerrville, in high hopes that he might do some work with the animals at Utopia Rescue Ranch. He shared some of their background being homeless, stray, and traumatized, perhaps. I thought, this could be a cathartic experience. These hopes were dashed quite early, however. My evacuee, so he informed me as he proceeded to decimate my liquor cabinet, did not believe in work. The credo of his flock, the Black Mardi Gras Indians of New Orleans, was "Always for Pleasure." This did not bode well, I thought, but trying to tell a homeless person to go home is almost like trying to run for governor of Texas as an independent. In the days, weeks, and years to come, Goat seemed to become happier and happier while I began to wake up every morning in a black, suicidal rage. But I'm getting a bit ahead of myself. Let's go back to early times, and I don't mean the whiskey. That was already gone.

If you're going to be an evacuee, I told Goat, you've got to dress like an evacuee. We went through my wardrobe of eclectic, perhaps over-the-top items, many of which I'd hung on to for sentimental reasons. Almost all of them seemed to fit Goat well, so I said, "Take what you like," and he did. He cut such a fine figure, indeed, that when the *Kerrville Times* interviewed him, they put his large photo on page one, wearing all of my clothes from head to toe, including rattlesnake boots with the rattlers' heads still attached. I wasn't really envious; it was just a bit unnerving watching Goat strut around the house drinking beer for breakfast in my favorite bathrobe (given to me by Miss Texas 1987) with his slothful scrotum hanging out while singing "Big Balls in Cowtown."

Then there was the matter of the telephone. Since I've always believed the Internet to be the work of Satan, the phone remained my lifeline to the world, especially in the heated last months of the gubernatorial race. Goat was monopolizing it like a one-man Jerry Lewis telethon. Not only were most of the calls and messages seemingly for him, but he was also racking up phone bills during all hours of the night, calling other victims of the hurricane as well as his many musician friends.

I hated to be an insensitive host, but I needed the phone as well. The last time I'd checked, I was still running for governor and besides, Cousin Nancy (of Utopia Rescue Ranch) and I had been working frantically to save twenty-four greyhounds trapped in a New Orleans attic by rising floodwaters. Now Goat began a frenetic series of calls to Dr. John, the Neville Brothers, Levon Helm, and many other musical luminaries, telling them Kinky was bringing twenty-four greyhounds out of New Orleans. As Goat yapped on and on, I confess to have been basking somewhat in the sunlight of my good works. The truth, unfortunately, did not manifest itself for several more days when Goat turned to me in my favorite Billy Joe Shaver T-shirt and said, "When are the greyhounds getting here?"

"We're working on it," I said. "Cousin Nancy's gotta make room at the Rescue Ranch for twenty-four more dogs."

"The greyhounds are dogs?" said Goat, removing my reading glasses from his nose in astonishment.

"Yes, Goat," I said patiently. "They're dogs."

"Jesus with jugs," said Goat. "I thought they were buses."

Things went downhill from there. The care and feeding of Goat became more all-consuming, tedious, and expensive with each passing week. Not that Goat wasn't a soulful, talented, well-intentioned man—not to mention, a man of the cloth—it was just that the cloth, in his case, was a little coarse. It was not unusual for him to drink a case of beer a day. At dinner parties and restaurants he would sometimes take his teeth out and make loud, obnoxious spitting and farting noises into his hands, creating a New Orleans beat-box. He often would endlessly describe sexual desires toward women in television commercials, declaring them "table" or "not table," and always providing running commentary on all bodily functions in colorful, though somewhat graphic language, such as "letting the possum out."

Don't get me wrong. Despite some rather glaring personality and hygiene drawbacks, there were, as well, many spiritual and charmingly human aspects of this modern-day holy man. First of all, he did not proselytize. This can be important when you're a Jew and you have a street preacher living with you. The reverend, indeed, proved himself to be not only eccentric but refreshingly ecumenical as well. During Thanksgiving, for instance, Goat opened the proceedings with what he called the Cowboy Prayer, i.e., "Matthew, Mark, Luke, and John, hold this horse while I get on." As an afterthought, the Native American essence of the man also manifested itself. Goat's Indian Thanksgiving Prayer went as follows: "Thanks for nothing."

When Goat was not on the phone at my desk, he busied himself sitting in my chair, wearing a terrific Hawaiian shirt I'd forgotten I had, drinking beer, and watching the History Channel with almost pathological persistence. He moved so little, I worried, indeed, that Goat might himself evolve into an historical artifact. I had never personally been responsible for the health, education, and welfare of an evacuee, and given the fact that he might well have been traumatized by the experience, I still did not see how the therapy of sleeping, drinking beer, and watching the History Channel was ever going to get Goat off his ass and back to New Orleans. It was time for tough love.

I assigned Goat the daunting task of being the nanny for my five dogs, the Friedmans. Some say the Friedmans are spoiled rotten and very difficult, demanding dogs, but this is not precisely true. They are merely older dogs who, like older people, have become set in their ways. Soon the Friedmans could be seen following Goat like a flock over the hills and valleys of the ranch. Perky, Mr. Magoo, Brownie, Chumley, and Fly all seemed to be quite fond of Goat and to accept him, more or less, as their spiritual leader. Goat himself fed this religious fervor by dressing the part. Wearing my black Willie Nelson sweatshirt with the hood over his head and carrying a large staff, he looked like a cross between a biblical shepherd and the grim reaper.

Using his New Orleans background, Goat soon began cooking for the Friedmans as well. One dish that seemed to really catch on, he named the "Triple Dragon." It consisted of bacon, chicken livers, and chicken gizzards. It wasn't long before the Friedmans, normally a rather cliquish clan, had welcomed Goat into the family. The one holdout was Mr. Magoo, who, while he was fond of Goat, would never permit him to sleep in my bed when I was on the road.

It was during this time of harmony and bonding that the fate monkeys struck again. Goat, who now was "wee-wee-weeing" to use his term, and letting the possum out approximately every five minutes, received yet another blow to his fragile physical constitution. Goat came out of the guest house one morning singing, "It's a double possum morning, Baby left me without warning sometime in the night." His mood seemed upbeat and positive. When I returned from town later in the day, he appeared almost as depressed as I had been since his arrival. He informed me that, during his fitful slumbers the previous night, a spider, apparently, had bitten him on the anus.

This amused me greatly, which only plunged my evacuee into deeper, darker depression. He took his Indian knife and cut up half of my aloe plants and applied this natural elixir directly to the spider bite. This Native American remedy soothed the wound but apparently only temporarily. Goat then proceeded to pillage what was left of my Jameson Irish whiskey, applying equal portions both rectally and by mouth. He claimed the healing process had begun, but in the morning I noticed the level of my Listerine bottle had dropped precipitously and the cap was loose, causing me to spill the rest of it over myself and the floor, and causing me as well to curse my evacuee, who'd just rounded the corner carrying a large flagon of Kona coffee and leaving, I noticed, a very small amount left in the pot. His spider bite was doing much better, he reported.

Any housepest will get on your nerves after two years. Particularly if the person has been a victim of what must certainly be considered one of our country's greatest modern tragedies. My evacuee indubitably did his best, not only cooking for the Friedmans but also serving up great New Orleans–style meals for both of us as well. He labored in the important task of West Coast Underassistant Hummingbird Man, helping his host with his only hobby, feeding the hummingbirds. You can't ask much more of your fellow man.

It wasn't Goat's fault that many times when I looked at him I saw before my very eyes, myself, a very clever form of identify theft. He would sit in my chair, drink my whiskey, smoke my cigars, watch my TV, wear my clothes, answer my phone, all the while talking about or performing bodily functions at rapidly increasing intervals. As for me, I would play a little desultory eight ball by myself and watch my life pass before my eyes. Having a man of the cloth living with you for a two-year stint, a man who drinks ten times as much as you, a man who incessantly vocalizes his sexual desires concerning Angelina Jolie, a man who often speaks in the argot of the gutter, can be an unnerving and eye-opening experience. But the same man recently buried a dead hummingbird with a full traditional ceremony poignant enough to very possibly bring a tear to the eye of any abiding Christian or Native American, and, in this case, one Jewish cowboy.

Then came the day, early in the summer of the second year, when Goat received an offer he couldn't refuse. He had been invited back to New Orleans by Xavier University to teach a course in—what else?—the Black Mardi Gras Indians.

Goat is gone now, and, I must say, I almost miss him. And I do sometimes wonder what might have happened if things had been the other way around. I do know that ours is a friendship that has been tested by time, adversity, and the fate monkeys. There may, however, be yet one more test to come.

Someday soon, Goat and I are planning a book tour together. He'll be promoting his new novel, a dark, disturbing book about Hollywood and witchcraft called *Shallow Graves* (available on

Amazon.com). I'll be flogging my latest masterpiece, a dark, dis-turbing book about the Texas governor's race titled *You Can Lead a Politician to Water, But You Can't Make Him Think.*

Will it be like old times when Goat and I get back together? Who knows? All I've learned is that it's okay to think you're a cowboy just as long as you don't run into someone who thinks he's an Indian.

CHANGE, PARDNERS

I never thought I'd see the day when I'd miss gun racks in the back windows of pickup trucks, but I almost do. I miss the old Texas Hill Country, where Adolph Hofner and the Pearl Wranglers performed at outdoor dance halls under the stars. I miss the days when cowboy shirts never had buttons and coffee with a friend was still a dime. Many of the stubborn, dusty, weather-beaten little towns, roads, trucks, jeeps, people, and animals are gone now. If I could, I would surround this magic kingdom with the fragile, freckled arms of childhood and keep it the way I remember it.

All through the fifties, the Medina post office had a sign on the wall that read DO NOT SPIT ON THE FLOOR. Today, of course, it would be unthinkable for anyone to spit on the floor; that would be almost as verboten as smoking. Medina is a small, dry town in a wet county that, to paraphrase my father, has been slowly dying for more than one hundred years—that is, until now. After standing strong through droughts, fires, and floods, Medina, along with much of the heart of Texas, is finally experiencing something that may change it forever. And as Joseph Heller once warned, "Every change is for the worse."

I'm referring, of course, to the fact that the whole world seems to be moving to the Hill Country. Some folks in Kerrville are celebrating getting a Home Depot, while yuppies in Houston and Dallas are running away from home as fast as they can. Where are they going? You've got it. "They all want a home, far away from the dome where the Cowboys and drug dealers play. 'Trade the smog and road rage for the stars and the sage'— that's what them developers say."

Texas Highway 16 from Kerrville to Bandera is one of the most beautiful drives you can take on this planet. By day, you'll travel through rolling hills, past green valleys and wooded canyons, over sparkling creeks, and under blue skies. By night, the stars will shine even brighter than all of the above. The hills protect us, and the canyons keep us cool in the summer, and the animals go about their secret business as they did before any of us were here. Yet even the natural beauty of the land registers in our consciousness only as another theme park of the modern mind.

There is a phenomenon that sometimes occurs around small towns like Medina that some call the "hidy sign" but I call the "Medina wave." A driver encountering another vehicle on the highway will casually, effortlessly raise his index finger from the wheel in a brief salute, acknowledging the other driver, the countryside, and life in general. The other driver, unless he's new to these parts, will respond in kind. Occurrences of the Medina wave diminish as you reach the outskirts of the bigger towns, disappearing almost completely as you travel farther, or at least that's how it used to be. With so many new people in the area, the custom is vanishing like the fast-moving tail of a comet. These days, you're just as likely to see drivers saluting each other with their middle fingers.

Like it or not, the peaceful, scenic, bucolic Hill Country is being dragged kicking and screaming into the twenty-first century. The old-timers, who once worked the land, who drove horses and carts over these hills, who still give directions by the bends of the river, now sit in little coffee shops in little towns and watch the parade of progress. The folks from the big city are escaping the madness, believing they are making a new life for themselves in the wilderness, possibly not realizing what the old-timers already know: that sooner or later, no matter where you go, you always see yourself in the rearview mirror.

Though the Hill Country has always been warm and friendly to newcomers, tradition demands that you be born here or dead before you're truly accepted. My family has owned and lived on the same ranch on the outskirts of Medina for fifty years, yet many of the locals still refer to it as the old Sweeney place. The Reverend Sweeney was a circuit preacher who lived here in 1921, drove a Model T Ford, and kept meat down in the well for refrigeration. In the twenties the Sweeneys traded the ranch for a restaurant in San Saba that went belly-up. Several years ago, five generations of Sweeney women came through on a road trip, and a lady close to ninety gave me a message to give to my octogenarian friend Earl Buckelew. She said, "Tell John Earl the little Sweeney girls came by to say hello." Rivers run deep in the Hill Country.

Yet some things go on as usual. Utopia has a new restaurant called Garden of Eat'n. Bandera continues to be the hell-raising Cowboy Capital of the World, with the Silver Dollar still featuring live country bands and sawdust on the floor, and the Old Spanish Trail still serving a chicken-fried steak as big as your hat in its John Wayne Room. The cedar choppers have all but disappeared from Ingram, and the disgruntled dentists

**"I think if I had it to do all over again, I'd sit on
this chair frontwards."**

keep pouring into Hunt. Some people brag about the new Kerrville Wal-Mart, but others are just as proud of a local institution with a memorable moniker: the Butt-Holdsworth Memorial Library. And back at the Medina post office, a Volvo has just driven up with a bumper sticker that reads "Free Tibet."

And the old-timers, like old dogs in the sun, are vaguely aware of traffic jams and conservative little towns like Fredericksburg now transmogrified into shoppers' paradises. Meanwhile, in hillbilly heaven, Slim Dodson sips his coffee, remembering a time long ago when the neighbors asked him why his cats were always going into their garbage cans. He told them, "They wants to see the world." Earl Buckelew is there, too. He recalls once showing some acreage to a guy from the city who wanted to know if the land was any good for farming or livestock. "No," said Earl. "All it's good for is holding the world together."

COMING OF AGE
IN TEXAS

Looking at the stars in the Texas sky, you couldn't tell the difference between now and then. But it's there, all right. It's the difference between a picture you carry in your wallet and a picture you carry in your heart. But hearts can be broken and wallets can be stolen and you know you've grown up when you realize how far you are away from the stars.

In the early fifties, however, when I was a child, I spat as a child, I shat as a child, and I wore a funny little pointed birthday hat as a child. I knew what every little kid knows about Indians, which, in a purely spiritual sense can often be considerable, and of course absolutely nothing about ex-wives. When I grew up and was finally released from the Bandera, Texas, Home for the Bewildered for rhyming words too frequently,

I knew a little more about Indians and still absolutely nothing about ex-wives except what Alden Shuman had once told me: "They'll stick with you through thick."

As far as Indians go, which is usually a good bit farther than ex-wives, I've collected about a million arrowheads over the years and made frequent visits to the Frontier Times Museum in Bandera, which is just down the street from the Bandera Home for the Bewildered. As well as countless Indian artifacts, the museum features a real shrunken head, a two-headed goat, and many other weird and arcane objects that delighted me as a child, and because of a rather unfortunate state of arrested development, continue to hold the same fascination for me now.

Children, it has always seemed to me, have a greater inherent understanding of many things than adults. As they grow up, this native sensitivity is smothered, buried, or destroyed like someone pouring concrete over cobblestones, and finally replaced by what we call knowledge. Knowledge, according to Albert Einstein, who spent a lot of time, incidentally, living with the Indians when he wasn't busy forgetting his bicycle in Princeton, New Jersey, is a vastly inferior commodity when compared with imagination. Imagination, of course, is the money of childhood. This is why it is no surprise that little children have a better understanding of Indians, nature, death, God, animals, the universe, and some truly hard-to-grasp concepts like the Catholic Church, than most adults.

Now, with the eyes of a child, I lit my first cigar of the morning and focused softly on everything that wasn't there. I'd survived half a fucking century on this primitive planet where the pecking of poison parakeets in the Northern Territories of Australia was the very least of our worries. I cast my mind back to when I was seven years old, sitting like Otis Redding on the dock at the deep water at Echo Hill Ranch in the Texas summertime. It was there and then that a rather seminal experience occurred in my young life, a small thing actually, but as Raymond Chandler often observed in his final stages of alcoholism: "Tiny steps for tiny feet." It was the first time I'd ever seen a man's testicle, unknowingly suspended, almost like a Blakean symbol, outside the lining of his fifty's-style bathing suit.

The man was named Danny Rosenthal, a nice man with a moustache and a cheery smile who probably had had his own problems then but, of course, as a child, these were not known to me. Danny Rosenthal was a friend of my father's and the only problem that I could see that he had at the moment was that a singular large, adult testicle was trapped like a dead rat outside the lining of his bathing suit. Danny Rosenthal was totally oblivious to this matter but it delighted me as a child, and because of a rather unfortunate state of arrested sexual development, continues to hold the same fascination for me now. Danny Rosenthal's testicle, indeed, hangs suspended like a sun over the happy memories of the last days in the lifetime of my childhood.

You don't see people's testicles hanging out of their bathing suits much anymore. Styles have changed, people have changed, the world's a different kind of place, they say. Instead of looking up at things we now spend most of our time looking down on them. Another reason we don't have Danny Rosenthal's testicle to kick around anymore is that people don't appear to have many balls these days. Balls, like imagination, seem to shrivel with age.

As far as Danny Rosenthal is concerned, I believe I remember my father saying that he stepped on a rainbow some years back. If that is indeed the case, I'm sure he's now swimming in the sky with his wayward testicle relegated in the way of all flesh to the shadows on the walls of Hiroshima. I've never told anyone about this small incident of a small child, least of all Danny Rosenthal, but I'm sure he's long past the mortal stage in which social embarrassment might have been incurred. I believe God watches over every testicle, even those that sometimes, quite involuntarily, stray from the herd. I believe that all of us will some day be swimming in the sky with Danny Rosenthal, or at least wind up in a bar somewhere singing Jimmy Buffet cover songs.

To my left and to my right the phones were now ringing. I puffed on the cigar a bit longer, then half dreamily picked up the blower on the left.

"Are you *there*?" said a voice.

"Where else would I be?" I said.

ROMEO AND JULIET OF MEDINA

n 1985, after the death of my mother, I left New York for good to seek shelter in the small towns that lay scattered about the Hill Country as if they were peppered by the hand of God onto the gravy of a chicken-fried steak. In New York, people believe that nothing of importance ever happens outside the city, that if it doesn't occur inside their own office, it hasn't occurred at all. My friends told me that I would be a quitter if I gave up whatever the hell I was doing in New York and went back home. One of the things I was doing was large quantities of Peruvian marching powder, and I now believe that leaving may have saved my life.

I'd had, it seemed, seven years of bad luck. One of my two great loves, Kacey Cohen, had kissed a windshield at ninety-five miles per hour in her Ferrari. My other great love, of course, was myself. My best friend, Tom Baker, troublemaker, had overdosed in New York. I'd come back to Austin just in time to spend a few months with my mother before she died. My dear Minnie, from whom much of my soul springs, left me with three cats, a typewriter, and a talking car. She wanted me to be in good company, to write, and to have somebody to talk to. The car's name was Dusty. She was a 1983 Chrysler LeBaron convertible with a large vocabulary, including the phrase "A door is ajar." At this time of my life, one definitely was. My mother had always believed in me. Now, it seemed, it was time for me to believe in myself.

After New York, you'd think Austin would be a pleasant relief, but to my jangled mind, there still seemed to be too many people. So I corralled Cuddles, Dr. Skat, and Lady into Dusty, and together we drifted up to the Hill Country, where the people talk slow, the hills embrace you, and the small towns flash by like bright stations reflecting on the windows of a train at night. As Bob Dylan once wrote, "It takes a train to cry." As I once wrote, "Anything worth cryin' can be smiled."

What is it about small towns that always seem to be oddly comforting? Jesus was born in one. James Dean ran away from one. While visiting Italy, my father once said, "If you've seen one Sistine Chapel, you've seen them all." This is true of small towns as well, except they're not particularly good places to get postcards from. ("Why would anyone want to live here?" somebody always says. "It's out in the middle of nowhere. It's so far away." And the gypsy answers, "From where?")

There is a fundamental difference between big-city and country folks. In the city you can honk at the traffic, shout

epithets, and shoot the bird at anybody you like. You know you'll probably never see those people again. In a small town, you're responsible for your behavior. Instead of spouting off, you simply have to smile and shake your head. You know you're going to see the same people again in church or maybe at a cross burning. (Just kidding.)

Another positive aspect of living in or near small towns is that they're breeding grounds for some of the most colorful characters on the planet. They're also good places to hear stories about snakes. Dry cleaning's cheaper than it is in the big city, and life itself perhaps is a bit more precious, always allowing for inflation. There is, of course, no dry cleaner in Medina. You have to go to Bandera. And if you want to rent a good video, you probably should go to Kerrville. I say this because the Bandera video store has *Kiss of the Spider Woman* racked in the section with *Friday the 13th* and *The Texas Chainsaw Massacre.*

Arguably Agatha Christie's greatest creation, Miss Marple hailed from the small English town of St. Mary Mead. In a lifetime of fictional crime detection, the sage Miss Marple contended that the true character of people anywhere in the world could be easily divined by casting her mind back to the people she'd grown up with. For instance, the shy peeping tom in London reminded her keenly of the butcher's son in St. Mary Mead, who'd been slightly off kilter but would never have harmed a flea. In such manner, she determined that he was not the murderer of the 5th Duchess of Phlegm-on-Rye. In other words, the small town, like the small child, often dictates the emotional heritage of the human race.

So, maybe there's not that much difference between small-town life and life in the big city. When I lived in New York, like most New Yorkers, I rarely ventured outside my own little neighborhood in the Village. I bought newspapers at the same stand every morning, frequented the same cigar shop near Sheridan Square, and hung out at a bar right across the avenue called the Monkey's Paw. Like most Manhattanites, I never went to Brooklyn, never visited the Statue of Liberty, never ascended to the top of the Empire State Building, and never took a ride on the Staten Island Ferry. That was all for the tourists, most of whom, ironically, were from small towns.

My old, departed friend Earl Buckelew, the unofficial mayor of Medina, always used to say, "Everything comes out in the wash if you use enough Tide." Yet there are tides that run deep in small towns, deep as the sea of humanity, deep as the winding, muddy river of life. There once were two lovers who lived in Medina: Earl's youngest son, John, and his true love, the beautiful Janis. Though still in their teens, it is very possible that they shared a love many of us have forfeited, forgotten, or never known. A love of this kind can sometimes be incandescent in its innocence, reaching far beyond the time and geography of the small town into the secret history of the ages.

In June of 1969, at a country dance under the stars, John and Janis quarreled, as true lovers sometimes will. They drove home separately. On the same night Judy Garland died, Janis was killed in a car wreck. John mourned for her that summer, and in September, he took poison on her grave, joining her in eternity. John and Janis were much like another pair of star-crossed young lovers, the subjects of one of that summer's biggest films. The town was too small for a movie theater, but that year, many believe, Romeo and Juliet played in Medina.

ABOUT THE AUTHOR

He's a dreamer who never sleeps. He's a soldier who never kills. He's a drinker with a writing problem. He's a cowboy who only rides two-legged animals. He's a writer of fiction who tells the truth. He's the only free man on this train.